CLASSIC DESIGNS FOR TODAY'S ACTIVE CHILDREN

KITTY BENTON

Illustrated, step-by-step instructions,
patterns, and techniques for
sewing daytime, nighttime, and partytime
clothes for busy boys and girls

Library of Congress Catalog Card Number:
85-80489

ISBN: 0-688-05684-9

Printed in the United States of America

First Edition

1 2 3 4 5 6 7 8 9 10

BOOK DESIGN BY LINEY LI

CLASSIC DESIGNS FOR TODAY'S ACTIVE CHILDREN

KITTY BENTON

Hearst Books • New York

Acknowledgments

Sometimes simple words of thanks are the only way to acknowledge enormous gratitude. This book could not have been written without the skilled and unwavering loyalty of Jane Stone, so thanks first of all to her, and to Jean Madden, who helped sew the samples. Kjrstn Barranti, Melissa and Gabriella Stone, and Marissa Witowski, patiently endured fittings. Marjorie Miller and the staff of the Library Media Services at the Fashion Institute of Technology, New York, offered invaluable help in costume research, as did the staffs of the New York Public Library; Cooper-Hewitt Museum library, New York; the New York Society Library, New York; the library of the Costume Institute of the Metropolitan Museum of Art, New York; the Los Angeles County Museum of Art; and the Delaware Art Museum.

Special thanks to Ira Bartfield and the photographic reproduction rights staff of the National Gallery of Art, Washington, D.C.

Interest and enthusiasm from O. F. Douglass, and the administrative staff and membership of The Smocking Arts Guild of America was welcome and inspiring.

Margaret Pierce, Inc., Greensboro, NC, provided the fine fabrics and laces for the Party Undies, the smocking projects, and the girl's viyella school blouse. The corduroy and gingham in the school projects is courtesy of G Street Fabrics, Rockville, Maryland, which also supplied the sleepwear fabrics and the velvets used in the party chapter.

I am indebted to Stretch and Sew fabrics, Springfield, Virginia, for materials used in the Active Play projects.

The production team headed by my editor, Joan Nagy, includes photographer David Arky, his assistant, Valerie Baker, art directors Cheryl Asherman and Liney Li, and Ian Gonzalez. Their collective professional expertise and joyous ideas made this project a pleasure.

I will always be grateful to Wendy Reider for her early support and patient tutelage, to my agent Berenice Hoffman, my husband Nicholas Benton, and to all my family and friends who plucked threads from my clothes and were patient with me throughout.

Last but not least, special thanks to Carter, Betsey, and Fred Smith.

◆———————————————————————◆

For my mother
Sylvia Weld Bigelow

my grandmother, Sylvia Caroline Weld,
who loved to sew

and my great-grandmother, Susan Edith Weld,
who loved the sound of children's voices

Contents

9

Acknowledgments

15

Introduction

19

School Days

*Start the day with sturdy school clothes:
corduroys and ginghams and no-nonsense seams.*

45

Party Dress-up

*Appliqué, embroidery, and traditional smocking
adorn special clothes for special occasions.*

75

Party Undies

*Fine fabrics and fine machine sewing techniques
combine to make a trio of luxury underclothes
for gifts or for wearing under party clothes.*

91

Active Play

*Knit techniques and modern fabrics
bring after-school comfort*

127

Summer and Sunshine

*Choose from three picture smocking designs:
dutch milkmaid, farmer and vegetables, or window boxes,
to create summer elegance for your boy, girl, or infant.*

153

Time to Retire

*Decorative seams enhance sleepwear and
sweet dreams after a busy day.*

177

A Library of Pattern Shapes

*Full directions for making every project in this book
from just seven basic pattern pieces:
bodice, sleeve, dress, and pants.*

191

Appendix

*Quick Grid Appendix; Converting Inches to Centimeters;
Mail Order Sources*

193

Index

Introduction

esterday's children were probably just as active as today's children, but perhaps were less noticeably so. Houses were larger, back yards were bigger, towns were smaller, life was simpler, and the adage "Children should be seen and not heard" had not yet been replaced by a click of the TV dial. Yet, even though styles of living change from culture to culture and from age to age, the basics of a child's daily life in any time or in any culture remain remarkably similar. Children go to school, play after school, dress up for special occasions, look forward to summer vacation, and finally, tired after a busy day of growing up, go to bed and fall asleep.

Thus, the chapters of this book are divided into segments of a typical child's day, grouped around clothes to accompany each activity. Highlighted sewing techniques and fabric choices complete the classic lines and easy fit of these simple designs.

GETTING THE MOST OUT OF THIS BOOK

As you leaf through the book you will see that it covers a broad range of sewing topics and includes general information on fabric handling, sewing techniques and tailoring, embroidery and smocking, fitting, and pattern-making. Some of this information may not be of interest to you. Perhaps you just like to sew occasionally or are sewing for a child who is not available for fitting. If so, you probably have no need for a wardrobe of basic patterns or for specific fitting information. You may wish to learn to smock, but embroidery holds no appeal. That's fine. The book has been designed so that the more adventurous or experienced seamstress may use it as an introduction to pattern-making and clothing design. But since each project in the book stands entirely on its own and can be made

Artist Pierre Bonnard used quick brush strokes to paint the snowflakes and jagged shapes between the children's scurrying feet to portray the age-old energy of childhood in his c. 1895 painting Children Leaving School.

without referring to any other sections of the book, feel free to pay attention only to what interests you and leave the rest alone.

SEWING TECHNIQUES AND FABRIC-HANDLING SKILLS

Each chapter begins with a short introduction succeeded by an explanation of the skills and techniques used in making the projects that follow. Taken as a whole, these fabric-handling recommendations and tailoring details comprise a short course in the tricks of the trade of professional dressmaking. A convenience for the beginner and a source, perhaps, of temptation for the experienced, these techniques may be successfully incorporated where appropriate in all your sewing projects—not just those included in this book.

ABOUT SLOPERS

If you look at the library of pattern shapes in the last chapter and then turn to the patterns for a few of the projects, you will see that all patterns in the book are derived from only seven basic shapes. These standardized pattern shapes are called "slopers" in the garment industry. Whether they are custom-fitted for an individual child or created from standard industry measurements, these slopers are the basis for every pattern in the book. A pattern for any given project is created by modifying the sloper to add or delete fullness, change the shape of a yoke or armhole, or increase or decrease length.

Since commercial patterns may be substituted for the patterns in the book, you may ignore if you wish all the information on how to use the grids, fitting a muslin pattern, and creating a permanent set of slopers. If, however, you would like to start building a wardrobe for your child, feel that you can never find a commercial pattern that fits properly, or would like to create your own designs, developing a set of slopers will be well worth your time.

HOW THE GRID SYSTEM WORKS

If, for whatever reason, you choose not to use commercial patterns, you will use the grid system to create your own pattern. (This same grid system is also used to make customized slopers, but more about that under "Fitting and Designing" below).

This is how the grid system works: Using your child's measurements (or the standard industry measurements listed in the

Quick-Grid Appendix), a heavy piece of paper is folded into squares of an appropriate size to create the grid. The number of squares on the paper grid duplicates the number of squares on the grid on which the pattern for the project is shown. The printed pattern is then copied square by square onto the paper grid creating, with the addition of pattern markings, a pattern that can be used to cut out your chosen fabric.

FITTING AND DESIGNING

If you decide that you do want to create a custom-fitted wardrobe for your child or if you are filled with your own design ideas and simply lack the technical knowledge or confidence to work them out, a permanent set of slopers is the best way to begin.

Permanent customized slopers are made according to the grid technique, but instead of using the paper pattern for cutting out your chosen fabric, the paper pattern is used to cut out a muslin pattern that can be fitted directly on the child according to the instructions in the last chapter. The shape of the adjusted muslin is then traced onto heavy cardboard or posterboard to create the permanent sloper. Style lines drawn across the slopers create yokes, panels or inserts, and a variety of sleeves and collars.

You'll see that each project pattern delineates the shape of the sloper with a dotted line and each modification to the sloper is shown as a shaded area within a solid line. Since grid patterns and sloper shapes are completely intercoordinated, you can work in any size you prefer and transfer any combination of shapes and concepts to your own design. For example, if you wanted to make big and little sister dress-alike yoke dresses, you could prepare a pattern for the big sister first. Using the concept of a yoke seam found in the School Jumper, separate the shift sloper into skirt and yoke sections. Next, borrow the technique of added fullness from the Party Bloomers pattern to enlarge the skirt panel. (You might even add enough extra fullness so that you could smock the dress in your favorite smocking design.) Choose any sleeve and a collar to complete the dress, perhaps even embellishing the collar with piping and lace as explained in the "Techniques" section of "Time to Retire." It would then be a simple matter to prepare a smaller grid and repeat the process for the little sister.

Slopers at the ready and the grid technique to assist you, your child's custom designed and fitted wardrobe will be as varied as your imagination allows.

 # School Days

ave you ever seen children ready for school in the morning? Hair combed, shoes tied, clothes pressed, faces shining? Coming home from school is usually altogether another matter. And even though today's schoolchildren don't run the risk of having pigtails dunked in inkwells, there are still spitballs, chalk dust, and muddy playgrounds at recess.

So it's still true to say children's school clothes need sturdy construction and sturdy fabrics such as corduroy and gingham that are up to the hard wear they will get during the day and the many washings they will get at home.

Corduroy, like its cousin velvet, is a pile fabric. Unlike velvet, corduroy alternates lengthwise ribs of pile with the plain background weave. The ribs are called wales, not after the country, but, curiously, after the raised pile portions which resemble the wales or welts that a whip can raise on the skin. Pinwale corduroy has wales as narrow as a pinpoint, wide-wale corduroy is self-explanatory.

In the sturdiest corduroys, the background diagonal twill weave supports the lengthwise pile. In all corduroys, the pile (derived from the Latin *pilus*, meaning "hair" or "fur") comes from a third thread looped into the weave with the filling yarn. After weaving, the loops are sheared to form the pile. The one-directional path of the shearing process trims the tops of the loops on a slight diagonal, causing changes in the way they reflect light. This is why pile fabrics appear to change color when they are not cut on a one-directional layout.

Whatever the fabric may be, active school children appreciate simple styles as well as comfortable fabrics for their school clothes. After all, comfort on the body frees the mind for higher purposes.

American artist Winslow Homer has tucked his initials into the practice alphabet on the schoolroom blackboard in this wry commentary on the administration of punishment to a guileless child called School.

TECHNIQUES
Sewing Corduroy

CUTTING. Determine the direction of the pile, turning to page 48 of the velvet party dress for help if necessary. Fold the fabric in half lengthwise with wrong sides together to prevent the pile from meshing on the inside, and lay out all pattern pieces with their tops facing in the same direction.

STITCHING. Use a size 11 needle and set the stitch length between eight and ten per inch. Loosen the upper-thread tension of the machine slightly and, if your machine permits, the pressure of the presser foot. (The universal pressure that sewing machine manufacturers claim is suitable for any number of layers and thicknesses sometimes causes the upper layer to "creep".) Sew *with the grain* wherever possible, pulling the fabric slightly taut behind the presser foot as you stitch.

1. Seam Finishing. Corduroy is bulky and needs to have each side of the seam allowance finished separately. Choose whatever method is most convenient for you.

SPECIAL OVERCASTING. Your sewing-machine dealer may carry the new type of machine that overcasts as it trims the excess seam allowance. This kind of machine is wonderful for corduroy and may be worth the investment if you sew frequently.

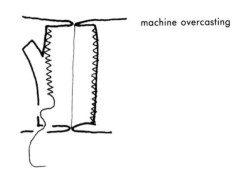

machine overcasting

MACHINE OVERCASTING. Loosen the upper-thread tension, set the stitch length at 12 per inch, and the zigzag setting at medium width. Stitch so that the points of the zig zag are ¼" inside the raw edge, then trim the excess seam allowance to the points of the zigzag.

stitched and pinked seam finish

STITCHED AND PINKED. Stitch ¼" in from the raw edge, then trim the remaining seam allowance with pinking shears.

---

2. Pressing. Steam is your friend and pressure is your enemy. Strive to saturate your seams with steam, then use finger pressure to spread them open or mold facings to the inside. When ironing flat on the board, iron from the wrong side and slide strips of adding machine tape or other paper under the edges of the seam allowances to prevent ridges from showing on the outside.

If you own a needle board for pressing velvet, use it under the corduroy to help prevent matting the pile. If not, a good substitute is a diaper rolled around a turkish towel. The best technique of all is a trip to your dry cleaner who often will press things at nominal cost and effort.

Sewing Gingham

1. The Flat-Felled Seam. This is actually a reinforced seam as the final row of stitches is also part of the basic construction. The seam is joined from the right side, one seam allowance is trimmed, and the other is hemmed over it. The yoke construction of the boy's shirt is particularly advantageous to the felled seam because of the bias grain over the shoulder, which gives "ease" for setting the flattened cap of the sleeve and for arm movement. Have you ever wondered how shirt manufacturers can afford all these steps in commercial production? They have specialized machines that stitch, trim, fold, and fell, in one operation.

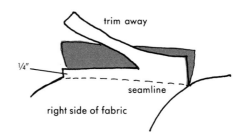

PREPARATION. With wrong sides together, align both pieces to be joined, raw edges and seamlines matching, and stitch them together on the seam line. Trim one layer of the seam allowance to ¼".

FINISHING. Press both seam allowances toward the trimmed side. Curl the larger allowance over, enclosing the smaller one, and edgestitch the felled edge to the garment.

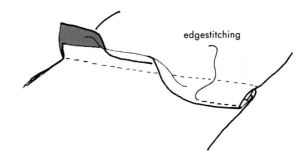

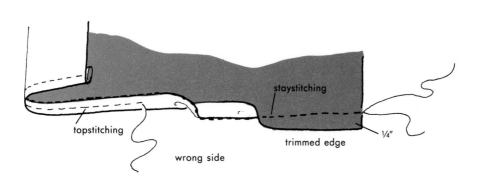

2. Narrow Topstitched Hem. (Also known as the shirt-tail hem.) Staystitch a fold line ¼" inside the unfinished edge. Trim the edge neatly and press the hem allowance upward. Grasp the staystitching thread ends in one hand and pull with the other to create a slight tension along the staystitching. This will help you turn the final fold of the hem to the inside.

Topstitch the hem from the wrong side leaving the needle in the down position through the fabric every time you stop to reposition your hands.

Boy's Gingham Shirt

The word gingham is believed to have been derived from a root word meaning *stripe*. Indeed, gingham as we know it alternates white and colored stripes of equal horizontal and vertical width to form the traditional checked fabric.

The best gingham is "yarn dyed," which means its checks are woven with contrasting threads. This ensures that the checks follow the grain of the fabric. If instead the checks are stamped with dye on the surface of the cloth after the fabric is woven, the checks will not always be straight throughout the bolt.

Polyester and cotton blends make a good fiber mix; the cotton is more comfortable to wear, the polyester is easy to wash. Sometimes the heat used to set the no-iron finish will force the threads off-grain, in which case even yarn-dyed gingham will be permanently askew. When in doubt, follow the grain.

Materials

44″–45″-wide checked gingham, 2½ times the shirt back length

Six sew-through buttons, ½″ diameter

Scraps of lightweight, press-on interfacing

The Grids

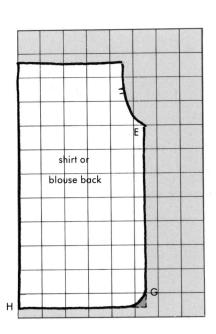

(If unfamiliar with the grid technique, see page 180, or substitute any commercial pattern that includes collar and yoke styling.)

Fold the appropriate grids and copy the diagrams square-for-square and point-for-point. Transfer any changes you have made in the A–H line to the center back of both the yoke and shirt back, and to the center front.

FRONT OVERLAP. Regardless of the size of the squares in your grid, extend the neck curve 2⅜″ beyond point A–A². Similarly, extend the hem 2⅜″ beyond point H–H². Cut the shirt front A²–H²–E–C–B–A².

23

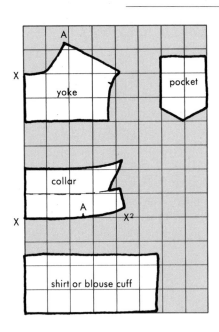

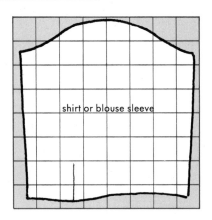

THE COLLAR. The A–X measurement should equal the neck curve of the yoke, less the ¾″ shoulder seam allowance. The X–X^2 measurement should equal the entire neck curve of the shirt front. Move the center back of the collar in or out as necessary to obtain the correct fit.

FURTHER FITTING. Alterations in length can safely be made to the shirt below the armhole and underarm seam of the sleeve. The armhole has already been widened and lowered for extra ease. If further alterations are absolutely necessary, be sure to make corresponding changes to the sleeve, following the basic guidelines given in the chapter A Library of Pattern Shapes.

Layout and Cutting

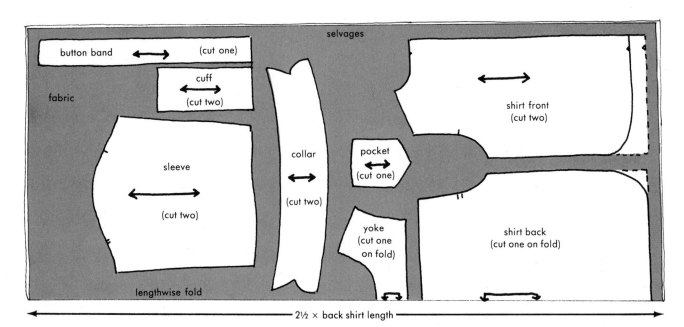

Fold the fabric in half lengthwise, wrong sides together, and lay out the pattern pieces according to the general principles of the sample layout, being sure to align the arrows with the lengthwise grain and placing all fold symbols against the lengthwise fold. Observe ⅝″ seam allowances except at the neck (¼″) and yoke seams (¾″).

Sewing the Shirt

1. The Fronts.

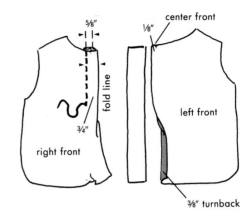

THE RIGHT FRONT. Establish a fold line ⅝″ beyond the center front. Turn the overlap extension to the inside and topstitch a 1″ double hem ¾″ inside the fold.

THE LEFT FRONT. Trim 2¼″ from the turnback allowance so the overlap extends only ⅛″ beyond the center front. Measure a fold line ⅜″ from the trimmed edge (¼″ inside the center front) and press the turnback, wrong side up, over the outside of the shirt.

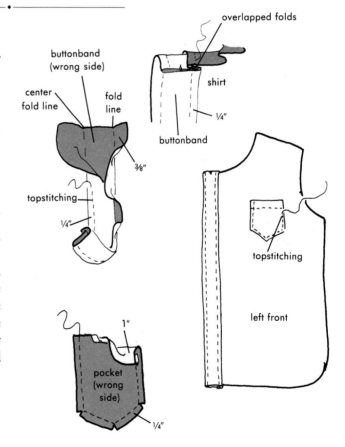

THE BUTTONBAND. Press a ⅜″ fold to the inside along one long edge, then fold the whole strip in half lengthwise, tucking the remaining raw edge envelope-style inside the pressed fold. Topstitch the center fold ¼″ inside the edge. Slip the buttonband onto the left shirt front, tucking the pressed folds into each other so that the raw edges are hidden.

Topstitch together all layers of the interlocked assembly ¼″ inside the folded edge of the band.

THE POCKET. At the top of the pocket topstitch a 1″ hem. Fold the ¼″ seam allowance to the inside around the outer edges, clipping the corners as necessary. Topstitch the pocket to the left shirt front midway between the button-band and the armhole at the level of the second buttonhole. Why the left side? Most people are right handed, so it is more convenient for them to use the dominant hand to put things in a pocket. If your child is left handed, you can strike a blow for left-hand lib and sew the pocket to the right shirt front.

THE HEM. To free the side seam allowance from the hem allowance, slash the shirt to the ○ and topstitch a narrow hem around the bottom of the shirt front. "Mock gather" the rounded area of the curve with moderate finger pressure behind the presser foot as you outline it during the preliminary topstitching.

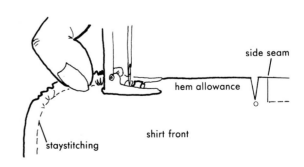

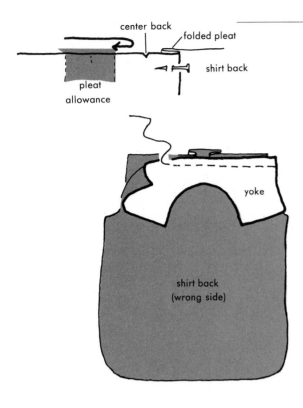

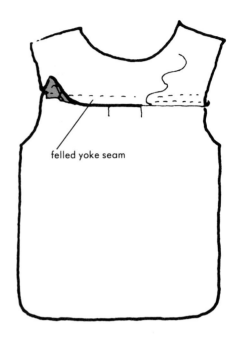

felled yoke seam

front yoke seam

2. The Yoke.

THE BACK YOKE SEAM. Fold and pin the sides of the inverted pleat to the inside at center back before joining the yoke seam. Trim the shirt seam allowance to ¼″ and the yoke seam allowance to ⅝″. Fell the seam downward over the shirt.

THE FRONT. Wrong side to wrong side, and with left front matching left yoke and right front matching right yoke, seam the prepared fronts to the yoke. Again, fell the seam downward over the shirt.

3. The Collar.

This slightly unorthodox method of collar construction is borrowed from the garment industry where five minutes of construction time saved can shave as much as three dollars from the retail price. Crisp fabrics like gingham render interfacing unnecessary.

PREPARATION. Staystitch the neck edge of the collar on the seam line. If the neck and collar seam allowances of your pattern are greater than ¼″, trim the excess from the neck seam and the outer edges of the collar.

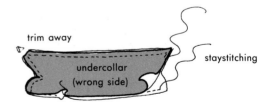

trim away

undercollar (wrong side)

staystitching

Seam together the outer edges of the upper and under collars ¼″ inside the outer edges. Trim the corners diagonally and clip the indentation at the onset of the neck band, as shown. Turn and press.

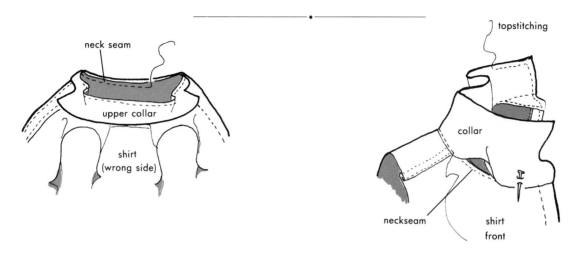

JOINING. Align the raw edges of the under collar and the shirt, and seam the under collar to the inside of the neck. Press the seam upward. Also press the remaining seam allowance of the upper collar to the inside, using the staystitching as a fold guide.

Pin the pressed edge of the collar to the outside of the shirt so that it just covers the stitching of the neckline seam, and topstitch all the layers together, stitching as close as possible to the fold.

Complete the tailored look of the collar by topstitching ¼″ inside the outer edges.

4. The Sleeves and Cuffs.

THE PLACKET. With a pin, mark the center of the sleeve at the wrist. Slash a 2″ placket opening in the back half of the sleeve midway between the center and the underarm seam. Face the slash with a continuous placket strip (pages 49–50), overlapping the finished strip toward the back.

THE ARMHOLE SEAM. Ease the sleeve into the armhole before joining the side and underarm seams to take full advantage of the flattened cap construction. After seaming, trim the sleeve portion of the seam allowance and lap the shirt over it to complete the felled seam.

THE SIDE AND UNDERARM SEAMS. Close the side and underarm seams in one continuous stitching, and fell the seam toward the front, stopping approximately 2″ above the hem curve.

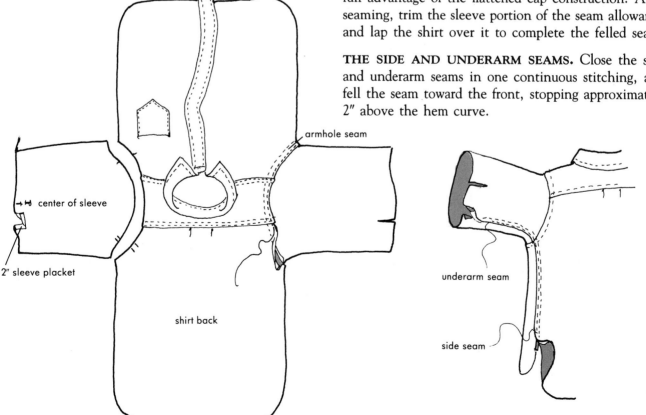

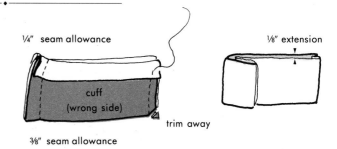

THE CUFFS. With right sides together, fold the cuff in half horizontally. Press a ⅜″-seam allowance to the inside of one wrist edge and a ¼″-seam allowance to the inside on the other, so that it extends ⅛″ beyond the first. Seam the short ends together, trim, turn, and press.

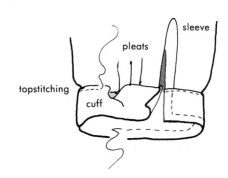

Tuck the sleeve into the cuff so that the extended edge of the ¼″-seam allowance is on the inside and the fold of the ⅜″-seam allowance is flush with the wrist seam line on the outside.

Fit the sleeve to the dimensions of the cuff and create extra elbow ease by forming a group of two or three small, closely spaced pleats midway between the placket opening and the center of the sleeve. Topstitch the cuff to the sleeve through all layers.

Finish the cuff with topstitching ¼″ inside the outer edges as you did the collar.

5. Finishing the Shirt.

THE BACK HEM. You have already hemmed the shirt fronts. Similarly staystitch the fold line for the back hem, easing the curve with "mock gathering," as you did the front hem.

Turn and finish the shirt-tail hem, blending the final fold into the felled seam allowance at the bottom of the side seam.

BUTTONS AND BUTTONHOLES. Make vertical buttonholes in the center of the buttonband, except for the top buttonhole which should be centered horizontally in the neckband. Center another horizontal buttonhole in the front of the cuff closing.

Finish the shirt by sewing the buttons to the right shirt front and the back of the cuff closing.

shirt-tail hem

Girl's Ruffle Collar Blouse

Girl's Ruffle Collar Blouse

The basic shirt pattern can be easily pressed into service as a girl's school blouse. Ruffles soften the neck and sleeve, gathering replaces the tailored pleats at the wrist and back yoke seam, and a simple, topstitched turnback replaces the buttonband at center front.

The fabric illustrated, which stands up to the hard wear little girls equally can give their clothes, is a wool-cotton blend: wool for warmth, cotton for washability.

Materials

41"–42"-wide viyella or similar wool-cotton blend, 2½ times the center front length

Six buttons

Scraps of lightweight, press-on interfacing

The Grids

Refer to the Boy's Gingham Shirt grids on page 23. The sleeve, cuff, and yoke are exactly the same. Trace the blouse front and back, including the shaded areas at the hem, once again planning a 2⅜" turnback extension

allowance at center front. Separate the collar from the band along the dotted line and cut only the band. It is not necessary to make a pattern for the ruffles.

Layout and Cutting

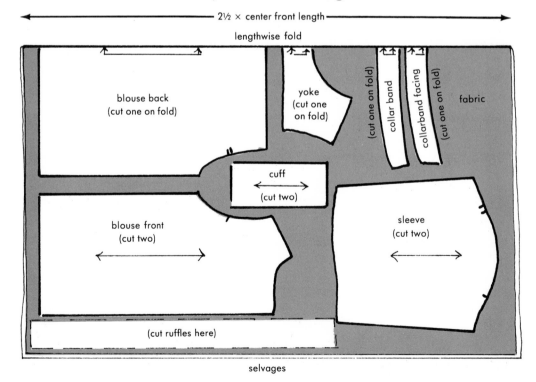

Fold the fabric in half lengthwise, wrong sides together, and lay out the pattern pieces according to the general principles of the sample layout, being sure to align the

arrows with the lengthwise grain and placing all fold symbols against the lengthwise fold.

Sewing the Blouse

Follow the general construction of the Boy's Gingham Shirt, with the following exceptions:

1. The Fronts.

THE CENTER FRONT. Establish a turnback fold line ⅜″ beyond the center front. Turn the extension to the inside and topstitch a doubled hem 1″ inside the fold line. If your fabric is stretchy, as some wovens are, reinforce the turnback with a 1″-wide strip of press-on interfacing, as shown.

THE POCKET. Follow the gingham shirt instructions for a tailored pocket, improvise a ruffle trim similar to the collar and cuff, or omit the pocket altogether.

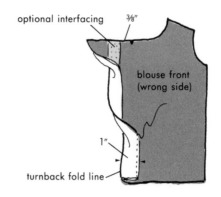

2. The Yoke.

Gather the blouse back with two rows of gathering stitches between the notches, and draw up the gathers to fit the back edge of the yoke.

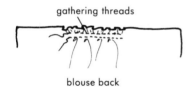

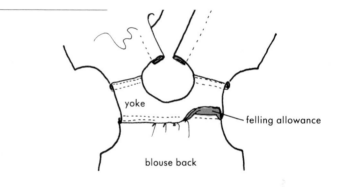

3. The Neckband.

THE RUFFLE. The width of the finished ruffle will be 1″ with a ½″ seam allowance. The gathering ratio for a nice full ruffle is two-to-one. Cut the ruffle strip on the lengthwise grain to double the length of the neckband and 3″ wide. Fold it in half lengthwise, wrong sides together; fold in the raw edges at the short ends and edgestitch them closed. Starting ¼″ inside the raw edges, stitch two gathering rows spaced ¼″ apart. The second gathering row will coincide with the seamline.

THE BAND. Staystitch the bottom of the neckband just as you did if you made the boy's shirt.

JOINING THE RUFFLE TO THE BAND. Gather the ruffle to fit within the seam allowances at the center front of the neckband. Stitch the front and upper edges of the band to the band facing, sandwiching the gathered edge of the ruffle between them along the upper edge. Leave the neck edge open.

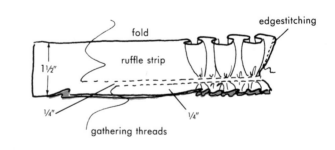

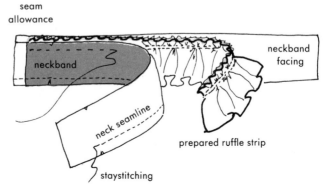

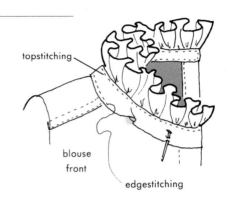

JOINING THE NECKBAND TO THE BLOUSE. Follow the instructions for sewing the collar to the boy's shirt.

4. The Sleeves and Cuffs.

THE SLEEVES. Prepare the placket and set the sleeves as for the shirt.

THE CUFFS. The width of the finished cuff ruffle is ⅝″. Cut the ruffle strips to twice the length of the cuff and 2¼″ wide. Fold and gather as for the neckband. Prepare the cuffs according to the gingham shirt directions.

Gather the bottom of the sleeve to fit the cuff, and baste the prepared ruffle over it, raw edges aligned and seamlines matching, before tucking the sleeve into the cuff and topstitching all three together simultaneously.

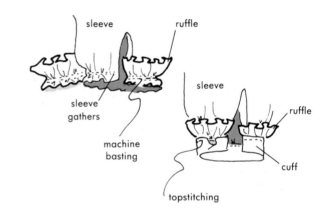

5. Finishing the Blouse.

THE HEM. Topstitch a ¾″ hem around the bottom of the blouse.

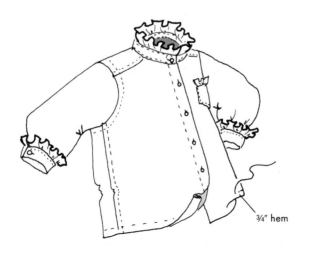

BUTTONS AND BUTTONHOLES. All the buttonholes may be horizontal if you prefer, but sew them to the right front blouse.

Why are boy's shirts buttoned left over right and girl's right over left? Once again, for right-handed reasons! Fly-front trouser closings open to the right to accommodate right-handed people. The left-over-right shirt closing is merely an extension of the center front line. However, it is basically more convenient to button right over left, so ladies, who until recently didn't wear trousers, simply arranged their buttons the easy way. Boys and girls both button cuffs from front to back, with button on the back and buttonhole on the front.

Corduroy Overalls

Corduroy Overalls

Buttons control the fit at the shoulder and waist on these sturdy corduroy overalls. A large pocket can accommodate snails and puppy-dog tails. Since the pocket straddles the side seam, placement is much easier if you join the seam and stitch the pocket before going on to construct the overalls.

Front and back linings face the neck, shoulder, and armhole, in one continuous seam, just as the lining faces the yoke of the Corduroy Jumper. If you choose wide-wale corduroy instead of the illustrated pin wale, place your scissors about 1/16" outside the edge of the pattern to compensate for the added bulk.

Materials

44"–45"-wide pinwale corduroy equal to 1½ times the shoulder-to-ankle length of the grid

Four sew-through buttons, 1" diameter

The Grids

(If unfamiliar with the grid technique, see page 180 for instructions, or substitute any commercial pattern for button-shoulder overalls.)

Since the overall is an extension of the Boy's Velvet Jumpsuit pattern, the jumpsuit outline is indicated, but the original sloper outlines are omitted to avoid confusion. Thus, the shaded areas indicate the relationship of the lowered armhole and neckline scoop to the jumpsuit, the dotted line between X and Y shapes the curved bottom of the facing pattern. The S–S² line indicates the leg line of the jumpsuit, but may also be used as a cutting line for a short-legged summer overall.

Fold the appropriate grids and trace the outlines of the front and back overalls following points A–B–C–E–L–M–N. Also trace the pocket, and tab. Transfer any adjustments you have made to the A–H lines of your original slopers to the traced grid.

If you suspect fitting problems with the armhole, neckline, or crotch depth, extend the shoulder tabs. The button-on fitting tabs at the waist should absorb

minor problems there. Trace the bottom curve of the front and back facing patterns from your completed patterns, as indicated by the dotted X–Y lines.

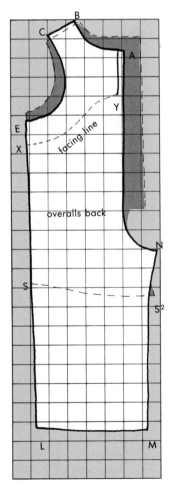

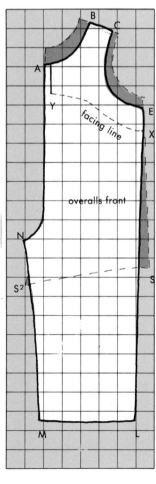

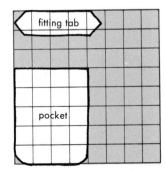

Layout and Cutting

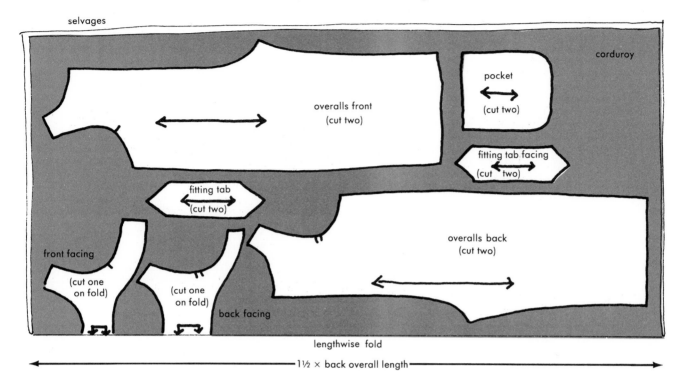

Corduroy must be cut with a one-way layout on the lengthwise grain of the fabric. Fold the fabric in half lengthwise, wrong sides together, and lay out the pattern pieces according to the general principles of the sample layout, being sure to align the arrows with the lengthwise grain and placing all fold symbols against the lengthwise fold.

SEAM ALLOWANCES. Allow ¼″ at the neck, armhole, and shoulder seams of the yoke, and ⅝″ at all others.

Sewing the Overalls

1. The Side Seam and Pocket.

PREPARATION. Prepare the pocket by overcasting and trimming the top edge. Staystitch the seam line around the outer edges, bunching the seam allowance around the curve by placing your finger behind the presser foot, as shown in the "Techniques" section of this chapter. Join the side seam of the overalls. Finish the seam as you choose and press it open.

TOPSTITCHING. Clip the bottom curves of the pocket, and turn the seam allowance and top hem allowance to the inside. Center and topstitch the pocket over the side seam at a level convenient for the hand, using the placement dots on the pattern as a guide.

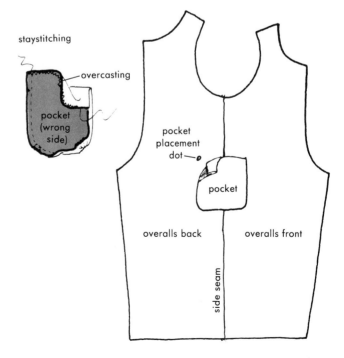

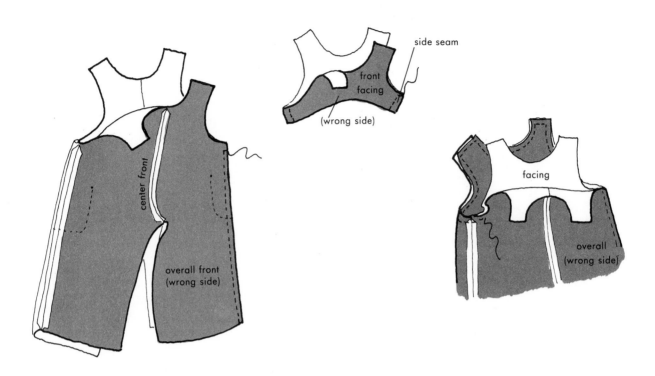

2. Facing the Neck and Armholes. Join the center front and center back seams of the overall and the side seams of the facings. Turn the facing right side out and leave the overall wrong side out. Slip the facing inside the overall, matching all raw edges around the armhole openings, shoulders, and neckline cutouts. Stitch the entire opening continuously from side seam to side seam 1/4" inside the raw edge. Clip the corners and curves, open out the facing, and understitch the facing to the underarm seam allowances before turning it to the inside.

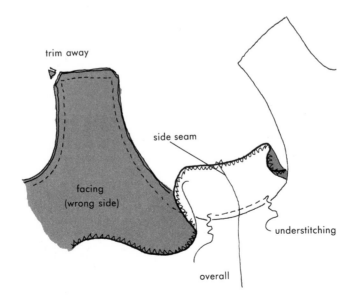

3. Finishing the Overalls.

THE HEM. Overcast the leg edge of the overall before closing the inseam and turning up the hem. If you prefer, consult the crotch seam directions for the "Hippo Bubble Romper" on page 122 and finish the inseam with a snap-tape closing.

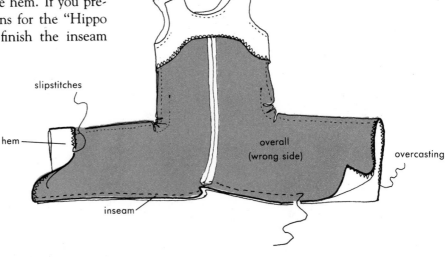

THE FITTING TABS. With right sides together and raw edges aligned, stitch the tabs to the tab facings, allowing ¼" seam allowance and leaving a portion of one long edge open. Clip the corners, pull the tab through the opening to the right side, and slipstitch the opening closed. Press.

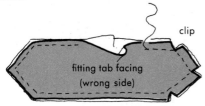

THE BUTTONS. For overall length, try on the overalls to determine the correct placement of the buttons on the back shoulder extensions. Determine the level of the waistline and sew the tab buttons to the front and back overall to fit the tummy.

THE BUTTONHOLES. Center a buttonhole to fit your button on each front shoulder and on each end of the fitting tabs.

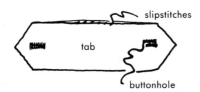

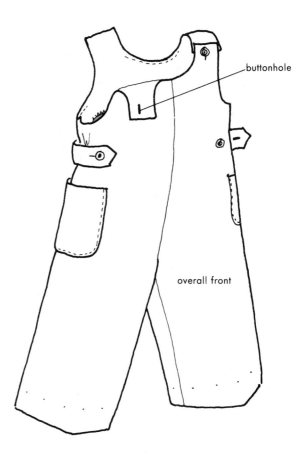

Corduroy Jumper

Box pleats are inserted on either side of the center front and center back to add fullness to the basic dress shape. The mid-armhole yoke gives a nice fit through the chest, the button shoulders and an extra hem allowance will allow for a year's growth.

You can always vary the design by omitting the pleats and gathering the fullness into the yoke seam, or pleat the skirt section and smock it just as you would a yoke dress. In any case, face the armhole and join the yoke seam as described in the instructions.

Materials

Baby-wale corduroy, fabric double the length of the skirt front grid measurement (flannel or cotton broadcloth are also suitable)

Face the yoke with self-fabric or ¼ yard contrast print or matching blouse fabric

Four ¾" sew-through buttons

The Grids

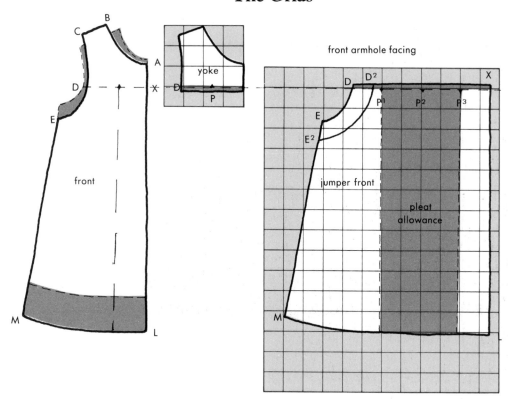

(If unfamiliar with the grid technique see page 180, or substitute any commercial jumper pattern with box pleats and a mid-armhole yoke seam.)

THE SKIRT FRONT AND YOKE. Notice the shaded hem allowance below the outline of the basic shift sloper, and the tab extension above the B–C shoulder line. The styleline D–X separates the yoke from the skirt. Transfer any changes you have made to the original sloper before tracing the jumper grids, then apply

the proportions of the shaded areas to your customized sloper.

Fold the appropriate grids and trace the yoke front pattern square-for-square and point-for-point, A–Y–P–D–C–B–A.

Trace the skirt pattern following points X–L–M–E–D–X, including the shaded area, between P^1–P^2–P^3, representing the pleat allowance.

Add ⅝" yoke seam allowance below the D–X line on the yoke pattern and above it on the skirt pattern.

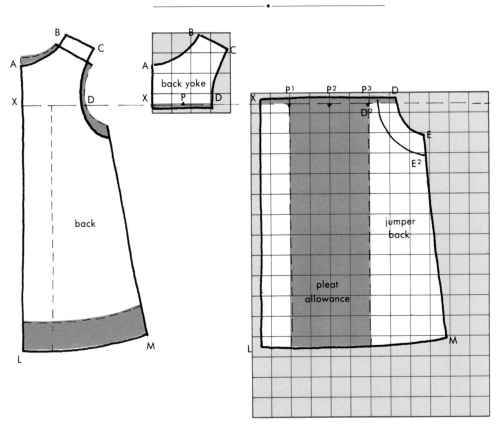

THE ARMHOLE FACING. Trace front and back facings as shown, D–D²–E²–E.

THE BACK YOKE, SKIRT, ARMHOLE FACING. Trace the outlines of the back patterns as you did for the front.

Layout and Cutting

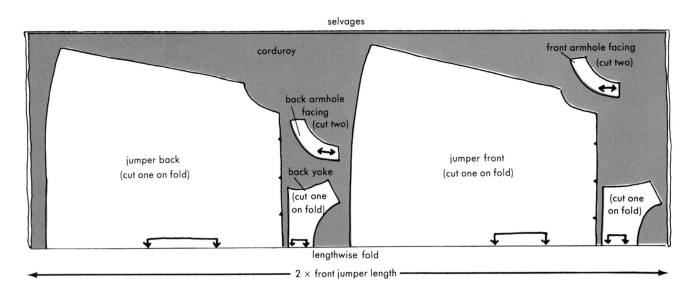

Corduroy must be cut with a one-directional layout on the lengthwise grain of the fabric. Place the pattern pieces on the fabric, aligning the arrows with the lengthwise grain of the corduroy and placing the fold symbols against the lengthwise fold, according to the general principles of the sample layout.

Sewing the Jumper

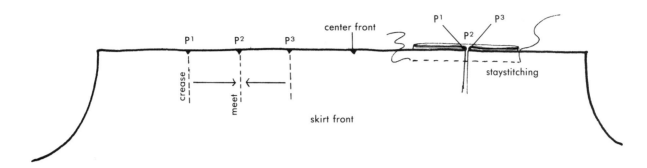

1. The Skirt.

THE PLEATS. Crease the fold lines at P^1 and P^3 to meet at P^2 in the center of each pleat, and staystitch them to the seam allowance at the top of the skirt front. Similarly pleat the skirt back.

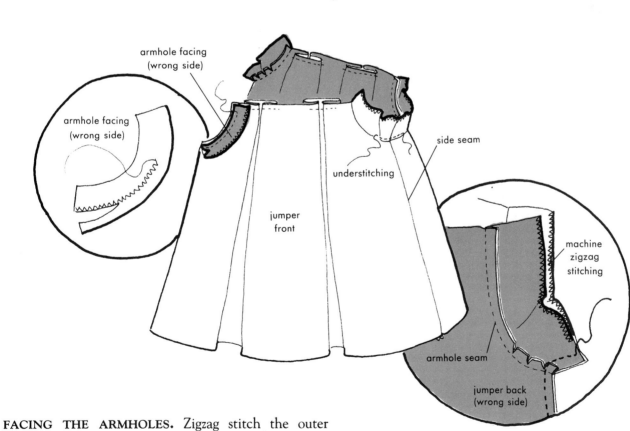

FACING THE ARMHOLES. Zigzag stitch the outer edges of the facing pieces ¼″ inside from the raw edge. Trim the excess fabric to the points of the zigzag. With right sides together and raw edges aligned, stitch the facings to the armholes.

Trim the seam allowances to ¼″ and clip them at intervals throughout the armhole curve. Spread the seam open so the facing extends into the armhole curve above the skirt.

THE SIDE SEAMS. Join the facings and the sides in one continuous seam starting at the outer edge of the facing and stitching over the armhole seam to the edge of the skirt. Finish the edges of the seam allowances as you choose and press them open. Understitch the armhole seam allowance to the facing before turning it to the inside.

2. The Yoke.

THE YOKE SEAM. Pin and stitch the yoke front to the skirt front, letting seam allowances extend beyond the skirt on both sides of the yoke seam. Carefully press up the seam allowance without matting the corduroy.

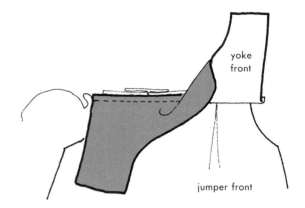

LINING THE YOKE. With right sides together, match the facing to the yoke. Starting and ending at the yoke seam, stitch the armhole, shoulder, and neckline cut-out in one continuous seam. Allow a generous ¼″ seam allowance across each shoulder and around the entire neck curve; taper the armhole seam allowance to meet the sides of the skirt at the yoke seam, if necessary. Trim and layer the seam allowances to a uniform width and clip them around corners and curves.

Turn the facing to the inside. Hem the remaining raw edge of the facing to the stitches on the inside of the yoke seam so that the skirt front is neatly sandwiched between yoke and facing. Similarly finish the yoke back.

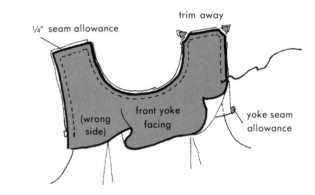

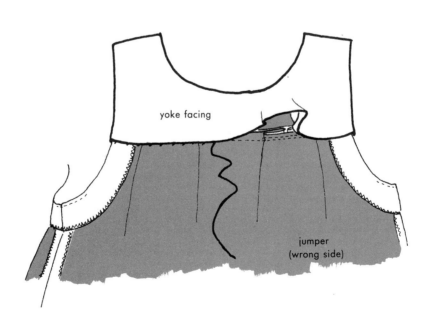

3. Finishing the Jumper.

THE BUTTONHOLES. Sew vertical buttonholes on the shoulder tabs of the front, starting ½″ below the edge of the tab. Sew the buttons to the back tabs, about 1″ from the edge, planning to move them closer to the shoulder next year to allow for growth.

THE HEM. Finish the bottom edge of the skirt with seam tape or overcasting. Turn up the hem allowance and catchstitch it to the inside of the jumper.

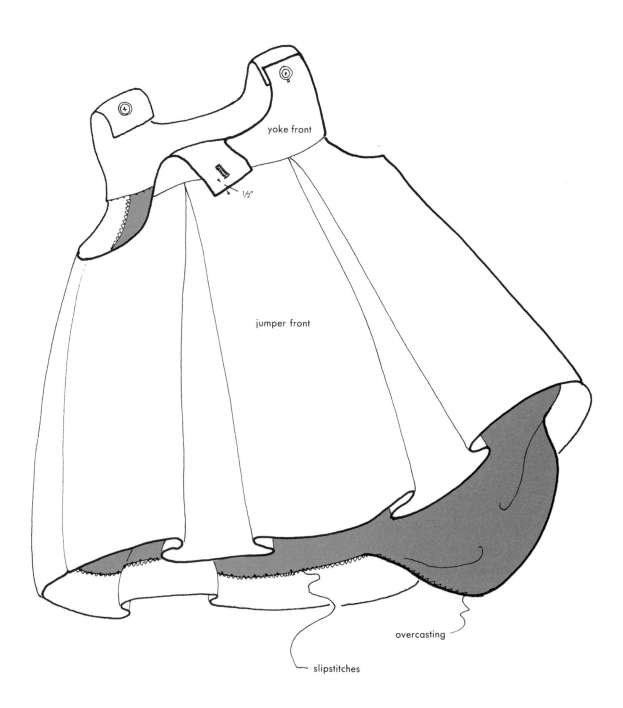

Party Dress-up

hildren wear neither makeup nor jewelry. Rather, ribbon and lace, eyelet and embroidery, smocking and appliqué are the jewelry of childhood—festive finishing touches of color and luxury that make the most of fine fabrics and enhance the beauty of the child.

Of course needle skills are not limited exclusively to children's clothes, or even to clothing at all. Diaries, account books, and paintings detail a priceless heritage of treasured tapestries as far back as A.D. 833, when King Wiklaf of Mercia hoisted a much-admired embroidered banner.

Needlework of all types reached its zenith in the latter half of the nineteenth century when every woman carried handwork in a reticule and complicated needlework patterns flourished in women's magazines, including patterns for tatting human hair into "hairwork," a practice still common in India where elephant hair is fashioned into beautiful bracelets.

The ancient Phrygians are credited as being the first people to spin a mass of gold (bullio) into coils of wire that could be sewn to cloth. The large coils, called bullion, could prevent a soaking in bad weather by wicking rain water away from the vulnerable shoulder seams of an officer's uniform, an idea that exists today in the form of epaulets.

By 1543, Princess Mary, a daughter of Henry VIII, was spinning her gold thread on a "little pirling wheel," a considerable improvement over earlier methods, which relied on two heavy men seated on swings kicking in opposite directions from a central tree to stretch out the wire secured to their waists with special belts. As the technique grew popular its function became decorative. "Pirled" wires were snipped into tiny lengths and embroidered on rich fabrics, in the manner of bugle beads, a technique that exists today in the form of the bullion knot.

All dressed for the party, perhaps having traded a nap for staying up late, this young lady in Lydia Field Emmet's 1911 painting Olivia seems to be enjoying a special moment of anticipation before joining the festivities.

Velvet Party Dress

The velvet dress has been a staple of dressing up since velvet was invented long ago in the Far East. This dress, shown here with the smocked collar, borrows its box pleats from the Corduroy Jumper.

If you don't make the smocked collar, you can always add a lace collar of your own, or embellish the neckline with a tidbit of gathered lace edging left over from the Party Undies, in which case, you might also stabilize the tops of the box pleats with embroidered florets.

Materials

42"-wide cotton velveteen, double the dress length

3 yards purchased matching bias binding, single fold

Three miniature pearl shank buttons

Optional: Lace: 1 yard of ⅜"-wide lace for neck trim
Embroidery floss: A few strands each of pink and green

The Grids

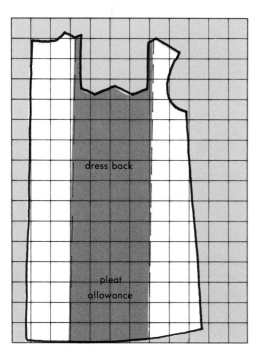

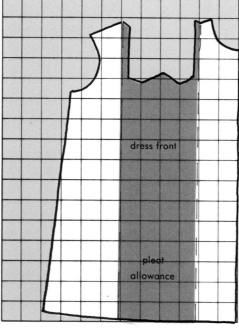

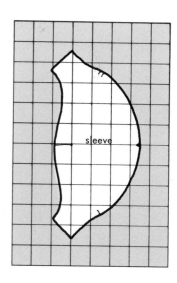

(If unfamiliar with the grid technique see page 180, or substitute any commercial dress pattern with box pleats and puffed sleeves.)

THE FRONT AND BACK. Fold the appropriate grids and trace the dress front and back patterns as shown, square-for-square and point-for-point, transferring any changes you have made to the original sloper as necessary and noticing the shaded area where the pleat depth allowance of four squares is inserted into the basic sloper outline. The pleats on both the front and back are sewn to a depth of three squares below the shoulder before being released.

THE SLEEVES. You may copy the puffed sleeve pattern as is without any worries of fit since a puffed sleeve can be adjusted to any armhole and any child, which may account for its continuing popularity.

Layout and Cutting

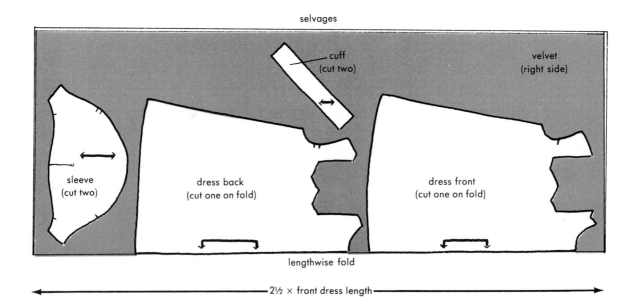

It is always important to plan the direction of the nap when working with velvet, but particularly so with black velvet. When the nap is facing up, the tiny, cut threads of the pile will absorb rather than reflect light, imparting a luxurious glow.

But how do you know which way is up? Fold the fabric in half lengthwise, wrong sides together, lay it on the table and smooth your hand over it to determine the direction of the nap. Stroking in the direction of the nap will feel smooth to the touch. Stroking against the nap will feel slightly rough and will show the path of your hand.

Place the pattern pieces on the fabric so that the pile feels rough when stroked from top to bottom. Lay out the pattern pieces according to the general principles of the illustrated layout, aligning all arrows with the lengthwise grain and all fold symbols against the lengthwise fold, smoothing against the nap from shoulder to hem.

Sewing the Dress

(If unfamiliar with the techniques for sewing velvet, refer to the techniques for sewing corduroy, page 20. The techniques are the same.)

1. The Box Pleats.

PREPARATION. Open out the cut dress front and, using a medium-wide zigzag stitch with fairly loose upper-thread tension, overcast the raw edges of the pleat cutout.

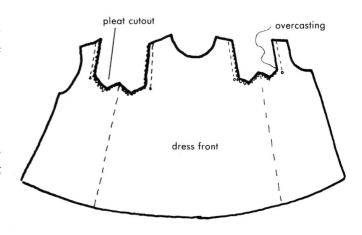

STITCHING THE PLEAT. Fold the pleat on the center fold line, right sides together, carefully aligning the overcast edges, and stitch from the shoulder to the ○.

Lightly steam open the seam allowance and, working from the wrong side, arrange the pleat over it so that the top of the inverted **V** shape is centered over the seam and the fabric falls evenly to each side.

Echo the **V** shape as you pin the pleat allowance to the inside of the dress below the ○. Then, working from the right side, replace the pins with tiny backstitches, no bigger than ¹⁄₁₆″, and spaced ³⁄₈″ apart. If you are careful not to pull the thread tight, the stitches will sink invisibly into the pile but will hold the top of the pleat securely in place so that it doesn't sag and spoil the shape of the dress.

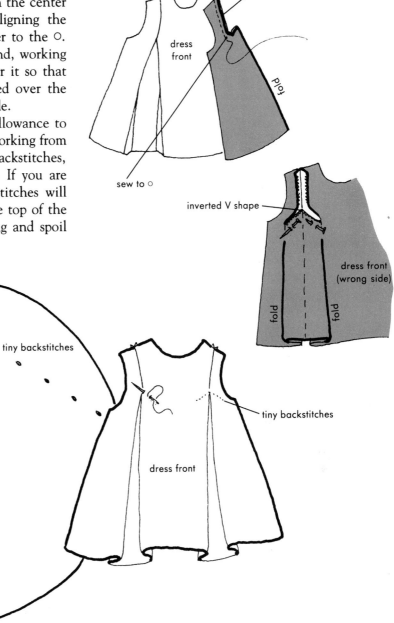

2. The Neckline.

THE PLACKET. Mark the slash line at center back to a depth of 2½ squares. Starting ¼″ away from the center at the upper left side, staystitch a V-shaped seam line around the edge of the slash, tapering to only a thread or two of seam allowance at the bottom. Leaving the needle *down* in the fabric, raise the presser foot, pivot, and stitch up the other side, tapering the stitching back once more to ¼″ from the raw edge at the top of the right side. Slash the opening to the point of the V.

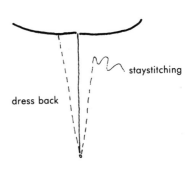

THE PLACKET STRIP. Cut a 1¾″ strip on the straight grain twice the length of the placket slash plus ¼″ for good measure. Staystitch (or imagine) a seam allowance ¼″ within each long side.

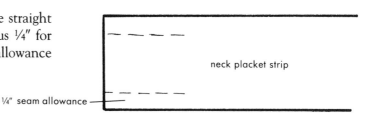

neck placket strip

¼″ seam allowance

SEWING. With placket strip underneath, right sides together, seam lines and top edges aligned, stitch the left edge of the slash to the right edge of the strip, allowing the ¼″ seam allowance of the strip to extend beyond the tapered allowance of the dress as you approach the bottom.

When the needle is exactly at the point of the slash, leave the needle in the fabric, raise the presser foot, and spread the slash so that the right side can be stretched over the rest of the placket strip. The fabric will bunch to the left of the needle. Push it behind the needle, lower the presser foot, and finish stitching the right edge of the slash, gradually widening the seam allowance back to ¼″ at the top.

Understitch the strip to the seam allowance from the right side before hemming the remaining free edge to the stitches of the seam.

Fold the right side of the finished placket to the inside so it will lap over the left side when closed.

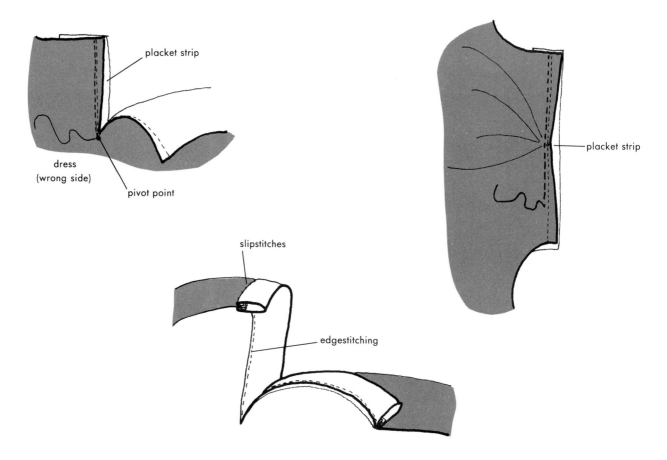

placket strip

dress (wrong side)

pivot point

placket strip

slipstitches

edgestitching

THE NECK FACING. Join the shoulder seams, finishing the raw edges with machine overcasting or any other preferred method.

Cut a strip of purchased bias lining 1″ longer than the neckline measurement. With a steam iron, pre-shape the folded bias strip to the curvature of the neck, unfold the inner curve and, right sides together, ease it onto the neck, once again matching the fold to the seamline, allowing a ½″ extension at either end.

Trim the neck seam allowance to ¼″ (if necessary) and slash it at ½″ intervals. Understitch the bias strip over the seam allowance, turning under the ½″ extensions at both ends. Secure the remaining long edge to the inside of the dress with invisible catchstitches.

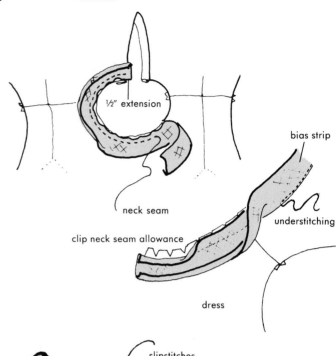

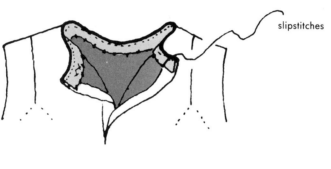

3. The Sleeves.

CUFF PLACKETS. Slash each sleeve from the hem to the ○, cut plackets twice the length of the slash plus ¼″, and sew them as you did the neck placket, turning the front side of the strip to the inside as a facing, and allowing the back side to serve as the underlap.

THE GATHERING. Sew two rows of gathering stitches between the notches of the sleeve caps, and between the notches and the placket on the bottoms.

SETTING THE SLEEVE. Pull up the gathers to fit the armhole and set the sleeves in the dress.

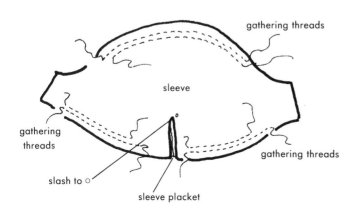

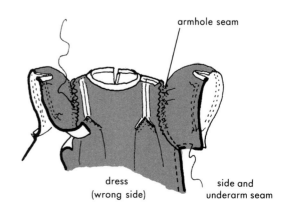

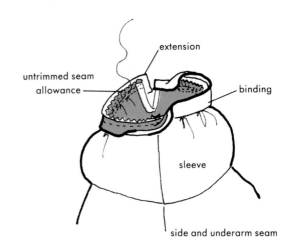

THE UNDERARM AND SIDE SEAMS. Close the underarm, side, and binding seams in one continuous stitching, and finish the edges as you prefer.

THE BINDING. Cut a 1½″-wide velvet bias strip 2″ longer than the child's biceps measurement. Pull up the gathering stitches on both sides of the placket so that each end of the cuff extends ½″ beyond the sleeve. With right sides together and raw edges aligned, sew it to the sleeve.

Hem the free edge of the binding to the inside (without trimming the cuff seam allowance which supports the binding from the inside and prevents "barber pole" wrinkles from forming), anchoring the hem stitches to the stitches of the cuff seam.

4. Finishing the Dress.

THE BUTTONS. Sew tiny buttons at the neck and sleeve closings, and handwork looped buttonholes to fit.

THE HEM. Face the hem with the seam binding and finish it with blind catchstitches.

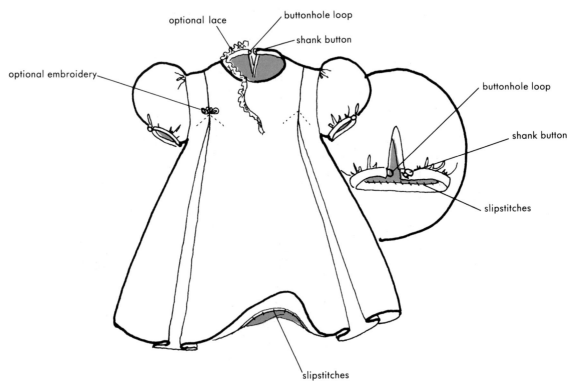

Smocked Collar

Smocked Collar

A simple rectangle of fabric and a few skeins of floss are all you need to make this beautiful collar. You can sew the collar permanently to the dress or mount it on a bias strip for versatility.

As with all smocking, once the fabric is pleated any pattern may be embroidered before removing the gathering rows, so you might want to explore smocking-supply stores for additional smocking design plates after completing your first collar.

Materials

½ yard 45″-wide batiste fabric

2 yards fine lace edging

1½ yards of 1½″-wide, double-faced, satin ribbon

Skeins of embroidery floss: 3 skeins peach; 1 skein each green, dark peach

Two shank buttons

Sewing thread

Sewing the Collar

1. Preparing to Smock.

CUTTING THE RECTANGLE. Fine batiste results in very fine pleats when pleated so the full width of the fabric is used in every size.

Remove the selvages and tear a 5″ rectangle. Pull the opposite corners diagonally, if necessary, to straighten the grain until all threads cross each other at 90-degree angles. Press.

THE PLEATING. Pleat the rectangle with nine gathering rows, by any preferred method. (If unfamiliar with smocking techniques, refer to the "Smocking Techniques" section on page 129.)

Cut a 14″ square of quadrille paper and enlarge the smocking guide, using a scale of one square per square inch. Grasp all the threads at once and pull up the whole rectangle to approximate the neck circumference.

Pin the top gathering row to the neck opening, allowing the rest of the pleats to radiate evenly from the center following the contours of the guide, adding pins as necessary until the center backs of the collar are flush with the center backs of the guide. Securely knot the ends of the gathering threads in three groups of four. Remove the pins and lift the collar from the guide.

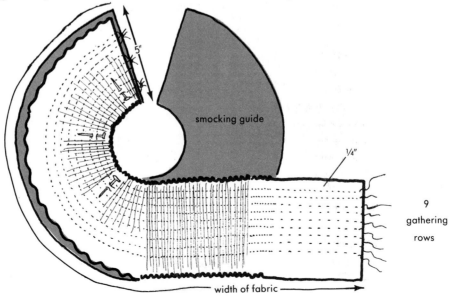

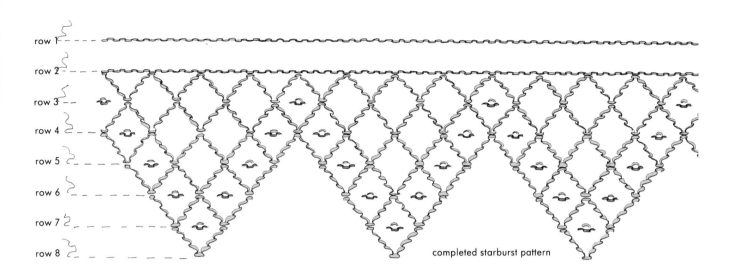

row 1
row 2
row 3
row 4
row 5
row 6
row 7
row 8

completed starburst pattern

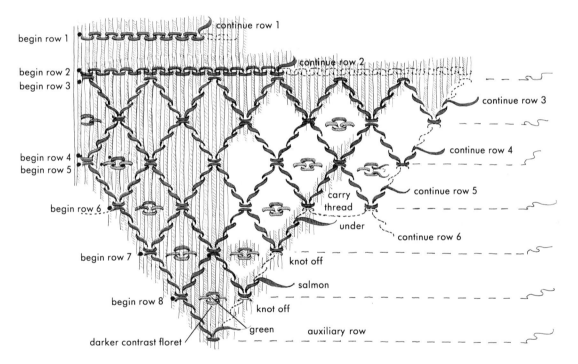

begin row 1   continue row 1
begin row 2   continue row 2
begin row 3
                               continue row 3
                               continue row 4
begin row 4
begin row 5   continue row 5
                          carry
                          thread   continue row 6
begin row 6   under
                          knot off
begin row 7
                          salmon
begin row 8   knot off
                          green   auxiliary row
darker contrast floret

2. Smocking the Design.

2. Smocking the Design. The top gathering row is unsmocked and falls within the neck seam allowance. The remainder of the rows are smocked in salmon, starting with two cable rows to stabilize the pleats. Rows 3 to 8 are successive rows of three-step waves to form the points of the star. Contrast florets and leaves outline the outer row.

ROW 1: Cable.

ROW 2: Cable.

ROW 3: Three-step waves.

ROW 4: Opposing waves to form diamonds.

ROWS 5–6: Continuation of diamond pattern.

ROW 7: Begin diamond points, omit every third wave.

ROW 8: Complete diamond points, knotting off thread between points.

FLORETS: Cable over, under, over with darker pink.

LEAVES: Cable over the middle cable of the floret with green.

3. Finishing the Collar.

HEMMING THE OUTER EDGES. Machine roll and whip the lace to the outer edges of the collar or invisibly topstitch the lace to a narrow hem, depending on your preference.

BLOCKING THE SMOCKING. Remove all the gathering rows, except the auxiliary row. Pin the collar back onto the paper guide and block it by holding a steam iron an inch or so above the fabric until the pleats are all even and the embroidery rests richly on top of them.

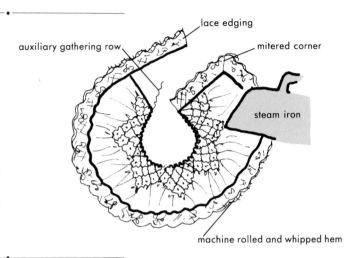

lace edging
auxiliary gathering row
mitered corner
steam iron
machine rolled and whipped hem

THE DOUBLE BINDING. Cut a 1½″-wide bias strip from collar fabric, 1″ longer than the desired circumference of the neck. Press the bias strip in half lengthwise, wrong sides together. Baste and stitch the bias to the auxiliary gathering row on the right side of the collar, ¼″ from the raw edge. Turn the long, folded edge up over the seam allowance and hem it to the stitches of the neckline seam.

THE TIES. Tuck the raw ends inside and hem the short ends of the double binding closed. Cut two 18″ lengths

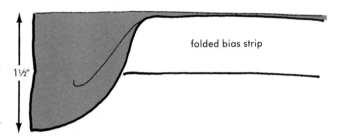

1½″
folded bias strip

of the ribbon, fold the ends under as shown, and tack them to the center back. Cut the remaining ends of the ribbon diagonally to prevent fraying.

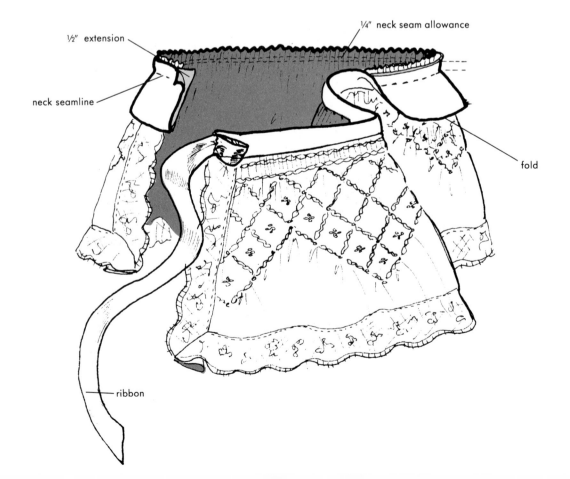

½″ extension
¼″ neck seam allowance
neck seamline
fold
ribbon

Boy's Velvet Jumpsuit

Boy's Velvet Jumpsuit

Active toddlers love bright, primary colors. The practical, one-piece construction of this red jumpsuit stays neat throughout the noisy rigors of birthday party games. Ice cream and cake don't phase washable velveteen.

Even fathers and older brothers, who claim not to care about clothes until the baby is dressed in something they consider sissy-ish, should approve of the bold colors and simple block shapes of the toy-soldier appliqué. Colorful, embroidered details echo the geometric triangles of the smocked collar; the uneven rectangle of the rhombus-shaped drum is mercifully silent.

If your little dynamo is still in diapers, review the snap-crotch technique on page 122.

Materials

42"–43"-wide, bright red cotton velveteen, 1½ times the jumper back length from shoulder to hem (Substitute bright red, yellow, or blue broadcloth for summer.)

Collar: ¼-yard white piqué

Purchased single-fold bias binding

Appliqué: Scraps of navy-blue corduroy, white piqué

Four white buttons, ⅝" diameter

Six-strand embroidery floss: scraps of blue, red, yellow

The Grids

(If unfamiliar with the grid technique, see page 180, or substitute any commercial one-piece jumpsuit pattern with set-in sleeves and Peter Pan collar.)

THE FRONT AND BACK. The jumpsuit pattern is developed from the basic bodice and pants slopers, which are indicated with dotted lines.

Notice the movement allowance between them at the center back, which provides extra ease to accommodate active bodies.

The side seam extension and dropped armhole, indicated by the shaded areas, complete the movement allowance.

Fold the appropriate grids and trace the outline of the jumpsuit pattern point-for-point and square-for-square. If necessary, transfer any fitting changes you have made to the original sloper before cutting the front pattern following points A–B–C–D–E–S²–S–Z. Similarly cut the back pattern including the button-opening turnback extension, N–O–P.

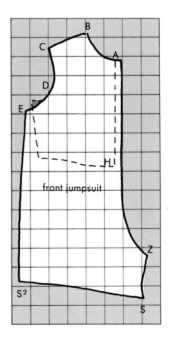

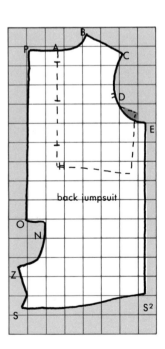

THE SLEEVES. If you made extensive changes to the original sleeve sloper, transfer them to the jumpsuit pattern before tracing the outline of the sleeve, $S-S^2-E^2-D^2-C-D-E$.

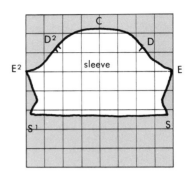

THE COLLAR. Even if you made no changes to the original sloper, it's a good idea to check the collar pattern against the jumpsuit neckline to guard against small variations in folding grids and printing accuracy. The distance from X to center front and center back of the collar should match the A–X distance of both front and back jumpsuit patterns.

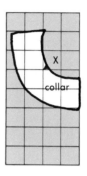

Layout and Cutting

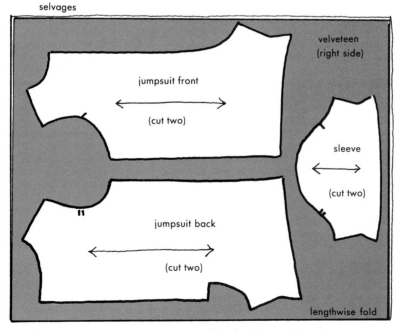

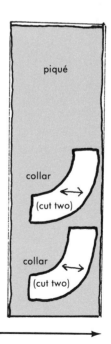

Fold the velveteen in half lengthwise, wrong sides together. After reviewing the instructions on page 48 for determining the nap of velvet, arrange the pattern pieces according to the general principles of the illustrated layout, placing all grain arrows on the lengthwise grain and all fold symbols against the lengthwise fold. Also fold the piqué in half lengthwise and cut the upper and under collars from the collar pattern.

The Appliqué

PREPARATION. Fuse a 4″ × 5″ square of corduroy and a 3″ square of leftover collar fabric to a piece of iron-on interfacing. Trace the actual-size appliqué patterns just as they appear in the illustration.

Cut the hat, jacket, and drum from blue corduroy (smoothing the nap against the grain from top to bottom), and cut the pants from leftover collar fabric. If you have a zigzag sewing machine, trim away all seam allowances; if not, clip the corners of the seam allowances and turn them under.

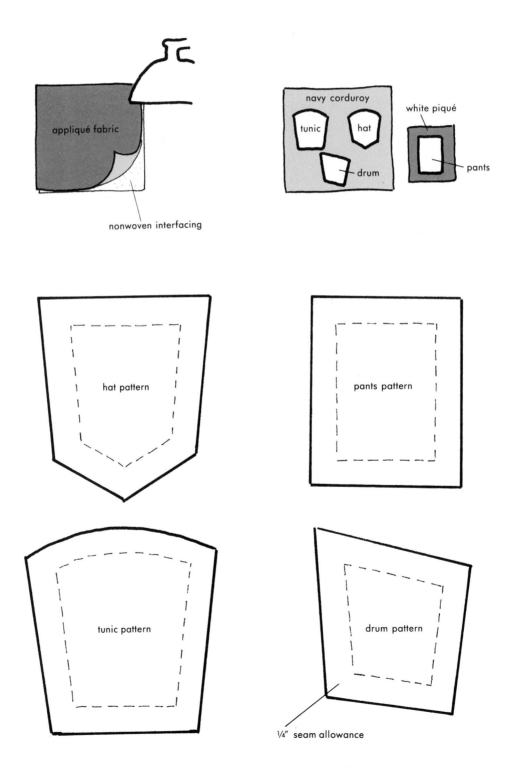

SEWING. Imagine a horizontal line across the jumpsuit at crotch level and a vertical line dropping from the armhole notch. Pin and baste the pieces of the soldier on the right side of the right front jumpsuit, positioning the bottom left corner of the pants at the intersection of the imaginary lines, as shown.

Set the machine at medium-width zigzag and satin-stitch length. If unsure of the correct appliqué setting for your machine, test a leftover scrap of fused appliqué fabric on a scrap of velvet to simulate actual sewing conditions before stitching. If you have a straight sewing machine, you may edgestitch or hand slipstitch the appliqué in place of the zigzag.

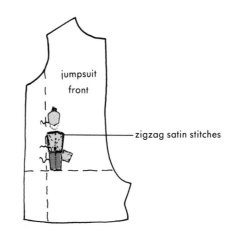

jumpsuit front

zigzag satin stitches

The Embroidery.

HAT: Brim band: Chain stitch, two strands gold.
Pom poms: French knots, two strands red.
Cockade: Turkey work, two strands gold.
Chin strap: Chain stitch, one strand navy.

TUNIC EPAULETS: Bullion stitch, two strands gold.
Braces: Chain stitch, two strands gold.
Buttons: French knots, two strands red.

PANTS: Leg definition: Backstitch, one strand navy.

DRUM: Banding: Chain stitch, one strand red.
Lacing: Chain stitch, two strands gold.

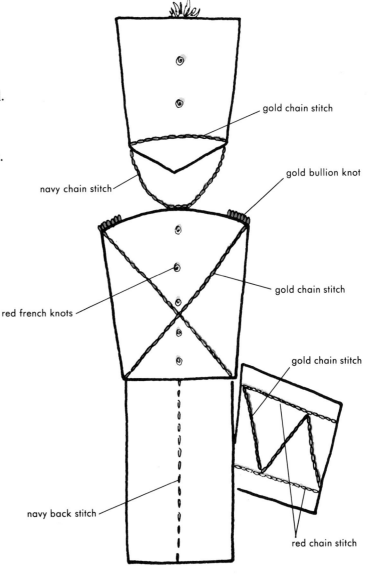

gold chain stitch

navy chain stitch

gold bullion knot

red french knots

gold chain stitch

gold chain stitch

navy back stitch

red chain stitch

Embroidery Stitches

There are literally thousands of embroidery stitches. Three variations of the chain stitch, two knotted stitches, and two amusing emphasis stitches are used in this chapter. All embroidery is best worked within an embroidery hoop. If you put the work aside for another day, remove the hoop to prevent stretching the fabric inside the circle.

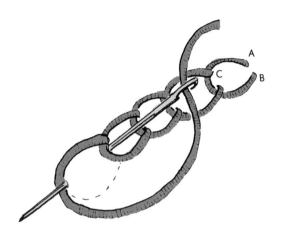

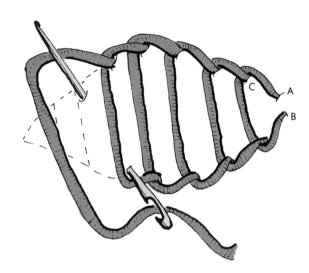

THE CHAIN STITCH. Bring the needle up at A, loop the thread, put the point of the needle in at B, and bring it out again at C to start the next stitch.

THE OPEN CHAIN STITCH. Widening the distance between A and B flattens the loop of the stitch and creates a ladder-like effect suitable for outlining and filling simultaneously.

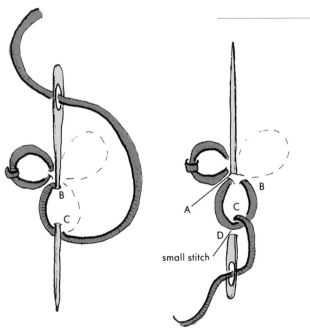

small stitch

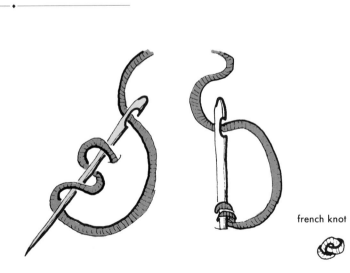

french knot

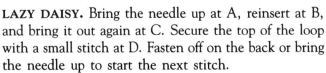

LAZY DAISY. Bring the needle up at A, reinsert at B, and bring it out again at C. Secure the top of the loop with a small stitch at D. Fasten off on the back or bring the needle up to start the next stitch.

FRENCH KNOT. Bring the needle up, coil the thread away from you twice over the needle, reinsert the needle right next to the beginning of the stitch, pulling the thread through the coils to tighten the knot against the fabric. Secure the thread on the wrong side or bring the needle up to start the next knot.

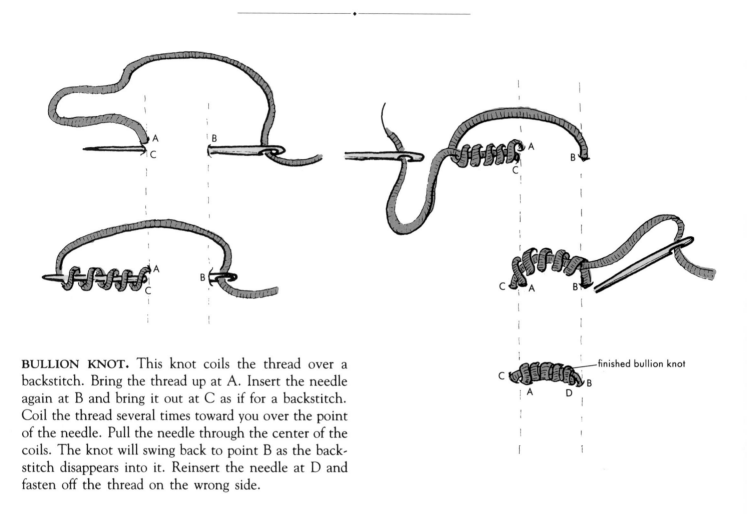

BULLION KNOT. This knot coils the thread over a backstitch. Bring the thread up at A. Insert the needle again at B and bring it out at C as if for a backstitch. Coil the thread several times toward you over the point of the needle. Pull the needle through the center of the coils. The knot will swing back to point B as the backstitch disappears into it. Reinsert the needle at D and fasten off the thread on the wrong side.

SEED STITCH. Scatter running stitches in a random pattern just as birds scatter seed beneath an outdoor feeder.

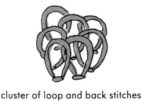
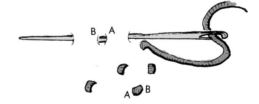

cluster of loop and back stitches

cut loops

needle

TURKEY WORK. Begin with a small backstitch. Take another small backstitch, but rather than tightening it, leave a ¼″ loop. Secure the loop with a third small backstitch. Cluster several stitches close together, cut through the tops of the loops and "worry" them with the back of your needle until they blur into a fuzz.

Sewing the Jumpsuit

1. Assembling Fronts and Backs.

THE BACK. Join the center back seam below the dot. Slash the seam allowance diagonally to the dot, machine overcast, and trim the seam allowance. Also overcast the edges of the button turnbacks.

THE REMAINING SEAMS. Join the center front and shoulder seams, finishing each side of the allowance separately with machine overcasting.

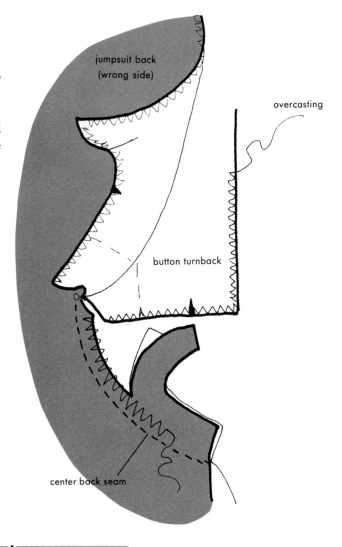

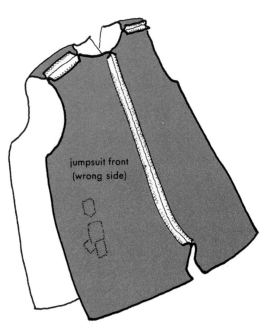

2. The Collar.

PREPARATION. Trim 1/16″ from the outer edges of a left and a right collar piece. With right sides together and raw edges aligned, ease the outer edges of the remaining collars onto them and stitch them together 1/4″ from the edge. Clip the corners, trim the seam allowances separately, and turn the collar. Baste the raw edges of the collars together within the neck seam allowance. This will cause the outer edge of the larger (upper) collars to curl slightly over the trimmed (under) collars, and will neatly hide the seam. Tack the two collars together at the center front seam line.

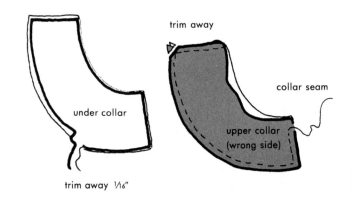

SEWING. Pin the collar to the jumpsuit, matching the back of the collar to the center back notch and the front to the center front seam.

Cut a piece of the purchased bias to fit comfortably over the collar. (No turnunder allowance is required, as the button turnback will finish the ends of the neck seam.)

Stitch the neck seam, sandwiching the collar between the bias and the jumpsuit.

Fold the bias out and understitch it to the seam allowance before hemming it to the inside.

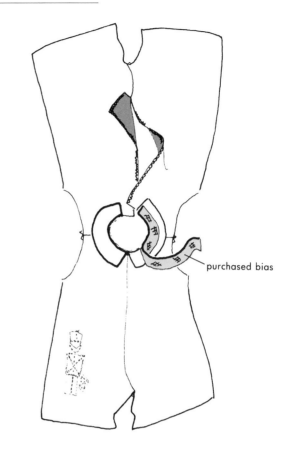

purchased bias

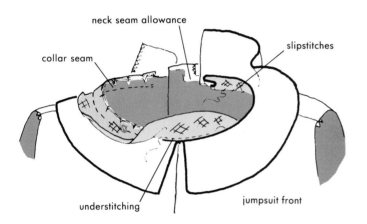

neck seam allowance

slipstitches

collar seam

understitching

jumpsuit front

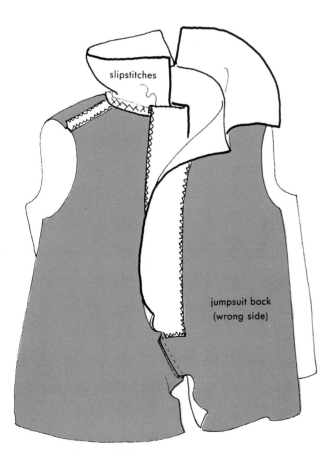

slipstitches

jumpsuit back
(wrong side)

FINISHING. Turn the button turnback to the outside on the fold line and stitch the bottom from the dot at the crotch seam to the fold line, as shown. Clip the seam allowance to the dot and fold the turnback to the inside. Tuck the neck seam allowance under, lap it over the collar, and secure it to the seam allowance with slipstitches, as shown.

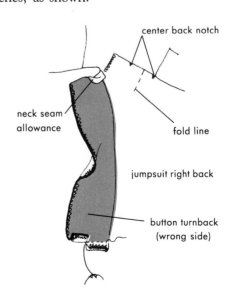

center back notch

neck seam allowance

fold line

jumpsuit right back

button turnback
(wrong side)

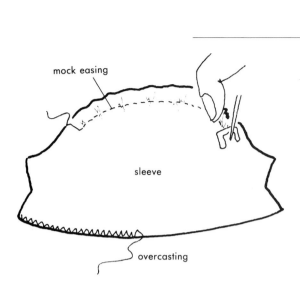

mock easing

sleeve

overcasting

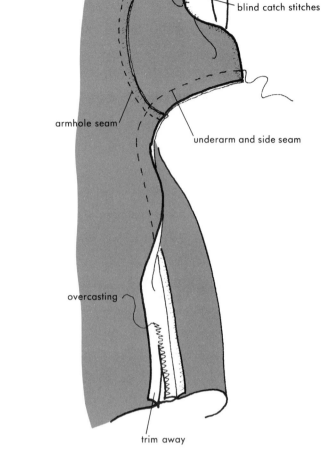

blind catch stitches

armhole seam

underarm and side seam

overcasting

trim away

3. The Sleeves.

THE ARMHOLE SEAM. "Mock ease" the cap of the sleeve between the notches and overcast the edge of the hem allowance. With right sides together and raw edges aligned, stitch the sleeve to the jumpsuit. Overcast and trim, or edgestitch and pink, the seam allowance to a width no more than ¼".

UNDERARM, SIDE SEAMS, AND SLEEVE HEM. Close the underarm and side seams in one continuous seam, finishing the seam allowances separately, as before. Turn up the hem allowance and secure it to the sleeve with blind catchstitches.

4. Finishing the Jumpsuit.

THE CROTCH SEAM AND HEM. With right sides together and raw edges aligned, match the center front to the center back and close the crotch seam. Overcast the raw edge of the leg, turn up the hem allowance, and secure it to the inside of the jumpsuit with blind catchstitches, as you did the sleeve.

BUTTONS AND BUTTONHOLES. Place the top button ¾" below the collar on the left back and the bottom button 2" above the start of the center back seam, spacing the other two evenly between them. Stitch corresponding horizontal buttonholes on the right back starting ⅛" to the left of center so that the left and right center backs will be flush after the buttons are buttoned.

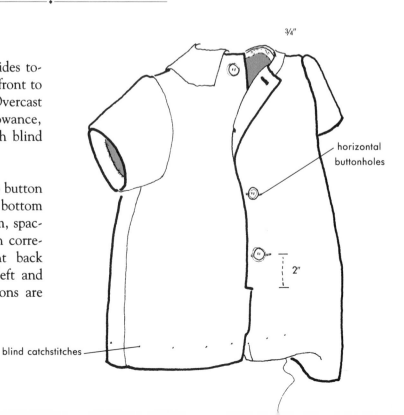

¾"

horizontal buttonholes

2"

blind catchstitches

Infant's Dress

Infant's Dress

The delicate subtlety of white-on-white is perfect for an infant's coloring.

Here, layers of fabric intensify the basic color to create the effect. White-shadowed tucks frame the dainty embroidery of the central bow knot, a tiny seam allowance frosts the scalloped-hem facing, gossamer webs of pure-white floss trace a garland of ribbons and flowers above it. Tiny ribbon threads a pearly gleam through the lace beading, echoing the horizontal definition of the hem. Lace and entredeux are the finishing touches.

Try adding extra length for a truly special christening dress or experiment with the equally beautiful effects of pastel shadings. Whatever your choice, use the finest materials available as a proper setting for your heirloom sewing techniques.

Materials

Approximately 1¼ yards of 42″–44″-wide finest batiste or lawn fabric

Two baby pearl shank buttons

1 yard of ⅛″-wide double-faced satin

1¼ yard, ⅜″-wide lace edging

1 yard entredeux

1 yard lace beading

Two-ply cotton lingerie thread (available at smocking-supply stores)

The Grids

(If unfamiliar with the grid technique see page 180, or substitute any commercial infant's dress pattern with front tucks and short puffed sleeves.)

THE FRONT AND BACK PATTERNS. Fold the appropriate grids and trace the front and back patterns square-for-square and point-for-point, noticing how the dotted outline of the original sloper falls inside the tuck allowance in the front and the shaded area in the back that represents the extra fullness created by the step placket. Transfer any changes you have made to the original sloper, as necessary, first noticing the shaded A–H extension to accommodate the infant's larger head proportion.

THE HEM FACING. Trace the hem facing pattern directly from the dress pattern, as shown, following points F–F¹–M–L.

THE SLEEVES. Trace the puffed-sleeve pattern as shown in the Velvet Party Dress grid.

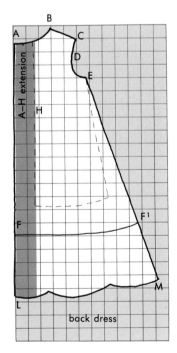

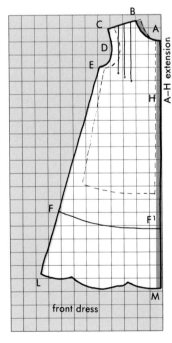

Layout and Cutting

Since it is easier to cut the front after the embroidery is worked, the solid line shows the front rectangle cutting line for the preliminary rectangle; the dotted line shows how the pattern fits within it.

Fold the fabric in half lengthwise, right sides together, and cut the pieces according to the suggested layout, matching all grain arrows to the lengthwise grain of the fabric and all fold symbols with the lengthwise fold, as shown.

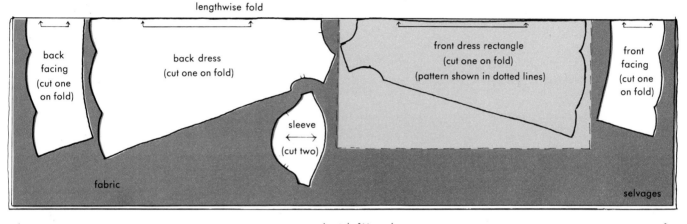

lengthwise fold

back facing (cut one on fold)

back dress (cut one on fold)

sleeve (cut two)

front dress rectangle (cut one on fold) (pattern shown in dotted lines)

front facing (cut one on fold)

fabric

selvages

approximately 1¼ yards

Sewing the Dress

1. The Front.

EMBROIDERING THE BOW KNOT. Trace the actual-size bow-knot design directly from the book onto a piece of tracing paper. Tape the paper to a large windowpane with plenty of light behind it; then tape the top edge of the dress-front rectangle over the paper with a piece of masking tape. The design, which will be clearly visible through the cloth, should be centered so that it will fall correctly when the actual dress front is cut.

Draw the design right onto the fabric with a special, water-soluble, embroidery-transfer pen (testing the solubility first on a scrap of fabric!).

Thread a needle with one strand of embroidery floss and work the design as shown, referring to pages 62–63 if unfamiliar with any of the stitches. Rinse away the pen marking and allow the fabric to dry. Gently press the finished embroidery, from the wrong side, over a turkish towel.

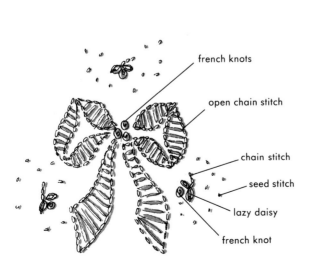

french knots

open chain stitch

chain stitch

seed stitch

lazy daisy

french knot

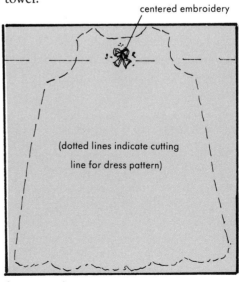

centered embroidery

(dotted lines indicate cutting line for dress pattern)

front rectangle

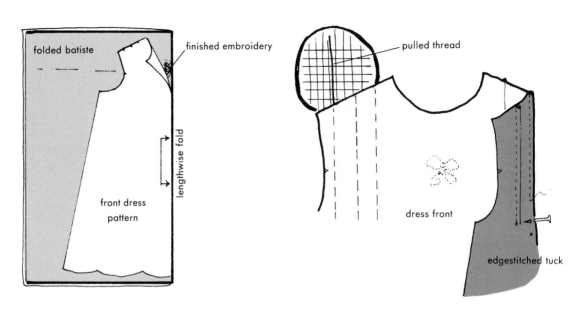

THE TUCKS. Fold the rectangle in half lengthwise, wrong sides together. Cut the dress front from the folded rectangle, matching the guide to the embroidery and the arrow to the fold, as the pattern indicates. Snip the fold notches at the top of the tucks with the point of your scissors.

Crease the fold, using a single thread of the lengthwise grain as a fold guide or by marking it with the water-soluble pen and a ruler. Edgestitch each tuck to the indicated depth.

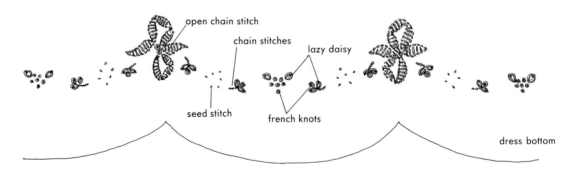

EMBROIDERING THE SCALLOPED GARLANDS. Using the windowpane technique, trace and transfer the garland design to the dress front 1½″ above the raw edge of the scallops, slightly expanding or compressing the design as necessary to match the bows to the tops of the scallops. Work the embroidery as indicated.

2. The Back.

THE STEP PLACKET. Slash the center of the placket allowance vertically between the center back notches to a depth of 4½″. Working from the right side, snip ¼″ horizontally to the right at the foot of the slash. Curl a ⅛″ double hem to the inside over the edge of the needle and secure it with slipstitches. Similarly snip ⅛″ to the left of the slash. Press the resulting ⅛″ hem allowance to the inside in a single layer without hemming it.

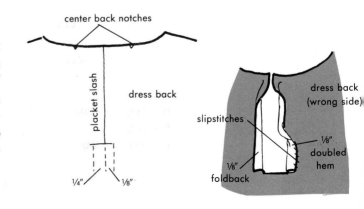

"Step" the right half of the back into a pleat over the left, matching the notches at center back and the folded edges of the placket cutout, as shown. Slipstitch the fold of the remaining free edge to the inside of the right back and secure the bottom of the step with an embroidered blossom or two.

Join the front to the back with tiny French seams at the shoulders.

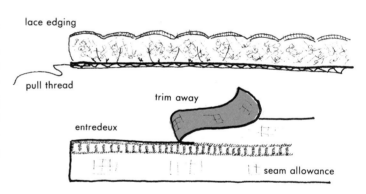

THE HEM EMBROIDERY. Mark and embroider the garlands above the scalloped hemline, as you did the front.

3. The Neck.

ASSEMBLING THE TRIM. Cut a length of entredeux 1″ longer than the circumference of the neck seam, and trim the seam allowance on one side to the edge of the stitching. Cut a length of the lace edging 2″ longer than the entredeux. Gently gather the excess by pulling one of the threads in the woven border until both strips are the same length. Whip the lace to the trimmed entredeux by hand or by simulated machine technique given on page 61. Press.

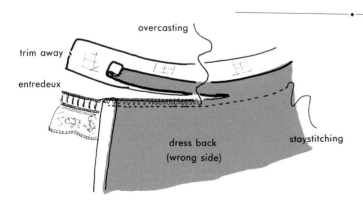

FINISHING THE NECK. With right sides together, staystitch the neck seam line of the dress to the stitching on the untrimmed side of the entredeux, allowing the seam allowance to extend beyond the raw edge of the dress.

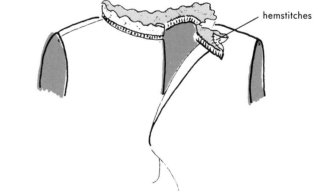

Trim both seam allowances at once to a scant ⅛″ and narrowly overcast them according to the fine-sewing techniques also on page 51. Turn in the ends flush with the sides of the step placket.

71

4. The Sleeves.

GATHERING THE CAP AND BICEPS. Set your machine stitch length to 18 per inch and the upper-thread tension to almost nothing. Stitch two gathering rows ⅛″ apart on either side of the seam line. Similarly stitch one row on the biceps seam line.

ASSEMBLING THE TRIM. Cut strips of lace, lace beading, and entredeux to fit the baby's arm measurement plus 2″. Whip one edge of the beading to the lace and the other to the trimmed entredeux, as before.

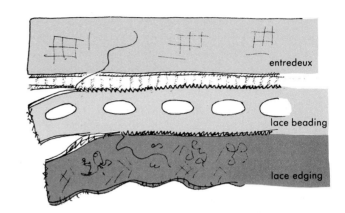

entredeux

lace beading

lace edging

SEWING THE TRIM TO THE SLEEVE. Gather the bottom of the sleeve to fit the assembled trim. Stitch, trim, and overcast it as you did before.

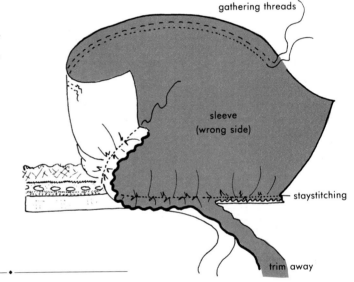

gathering threads

sleeve (wrong side)

staystitching

trim away

SETTING THE SLEEVE. Gather the cap to fit the armhole, matching the notches at front and back. With right sides together and raw edges aligned, stitch the sleeve to the dress. Trim the seam allowance to a scant ⅛″ and overcast it with narrow, zigzag stitches.

THE SIDE AND UNDERARM SEAMS. The side seam is an important part of the white-on-white effect and should be joined with a tiny French seam (see page 77, if unfamiliar with the technique). With wrong sides together, pin the entire length of the side and underarm seams together, carefully matching the intersection of the armhole seam and the trim on both sides. Stitch the preliminary seam a generous ⅛″ inside the final seam line. Trim the remaining seam allowance to ¹⁄₁₆″ before sewing the final seam.

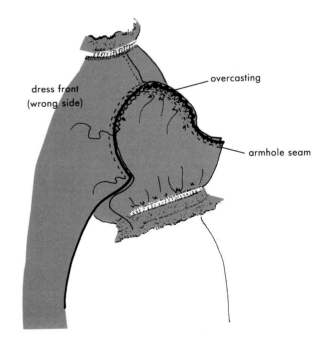

dress front (wrong side)

overcasting

armhole seam

5. Facing the Hem.

THE HEM FACING. Similarly seam the sides of the front and back facings with tiny French seams. Press a ½″ hem allowance to the inside at the top.

Slip the prepared facing, wrong side out, over the dress and, starting at the side seams and working toward the center, carefully align the scallops and pin them together. Stitch the seam ½″ inside the raw edge, trim the seam allowance to a scant ⅛″, and clip the points of the scallops to the stitching.

Turn the facing to the inside, taking care not to twist the hem seam, and press it over a padded towel so as not to crush the embroidered garlanding. Trim the hem allowance at the top to ⅛″ and slipstitch it to the dress.

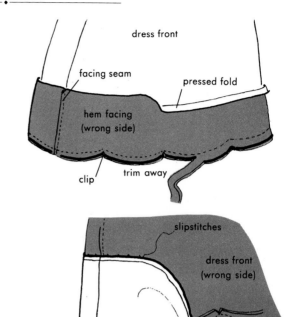

dress front

facing seam

pressed fold

hem facing (wrong side)

clip

trim away

slipstitches

dress front (wrong side)

hem facing (wrong side)

6. Finishing the Dress.

BUTTONS AND BUTTONHOLES. Sew tiny, pearlized, shank buttons to the center back on the left side, one just at the neckline and the other 1½″ below it. Chain corresponding buttonloops on the right side.

THE RIBBON. Starting and ending opposite the underarm seam, weave the narrow double-faced satin ribbon through the sleeve beading. Tie the ends of the ribbon into a bow at the starting point, trimming the ends diagonally to the correct length after the bow is tied.

ribbon

pearlized shank button

loop buttonhole

slipstitches

73

Party Undies

ny garment meant to be concealed from view is classified as "underwear."

In Elizabethan times, before modern plumbing and the idea of cleanliness being next to godliness, willow boards and huge cage-like petticoats called "farthingales" shaped the silhouette. Cotton chemises were worn underneath it all not so much for comfort, but to protect the elaborately jewelled velvets and richly embroidered silks from the filthy skin underneath.

The Victorians favored more frequent changes of personal linen, but had just as uncomfortable a silhouette. Starting as young as the age of three, boys and girls were corseted with stays made of steel, bone, wood, or tin, to shape both the waist and the character in the belief that a straight back and good posture indicated impeccable virtue.

In 1654, the Puritans passed laws demanding the forfeiture of any garment trimmed with embroidery or lace, and children donned homespun "linsey-woolsey" petticoats in rooms so cold that water used for washing faces and hands often froze in the bowl.

Some underwear is almost too beautiful to conceal. Puritans notwithstanding, a petticoat hem is an ideal spot for a beautiful trimming of lace, and even the straight-laced Victorians permitted ruffled, cotton pantaloons to peep fetchingly from beneath hoop skirts.

Cotton has always been a popular fabric for underwear. First known in Egypt and India, cotton is older than recorded history. Archaeologists have found definitive traces of it as early as 3000 B.C. and there are clues that cotton was known as early as 12,000 B.C. Later evidence from painted tomb panels shows that the Egyptians were thoroughly familiar with spin-

Flinging up one's skirt and showing one's underwear would have been considered a shocking act of rebellion in 1878 when American artist Mary Cassatt painted this scene. Fortunately no one is home except the dog, which doesn't seem to have taken offense.

ning, weaving, and even rudimentary processing of cotton fibers. Long before the days of the British Empire, early British travelers passing through India mistook cotton plants for wool plants and reported little lambs growing on trees. The English word for cotton is derived from the Arab word *kutn,* meaning "plant growing in a conquered land," which Arabian traders used to tell of cotton strands finer than the finest hair and cotton fabrics as soft as woven webs in the wind.

Other names for cotton use place names or people associated with refinements in its processing and weaving. Calico was first made in Calcutta. Mercerized cotton honors an Englishman, John Mercer, who discovered that cotton took on a high luster and accepted more colorful dyes after immersion in a bath of caustic soda. The fine weave of batiste is named after Jean Baptiste, a textile maker of the French town of Cambrai. Chambray is named after the town itself. Fine Swiss fabrics come not so much from the basic staple, plant, or fabric, but from the components of the refining and processing machinery. *Swiss* is actually a generic name for fabric that has been threaded through a series of heavy rollers and pressed to a transparent and lustrous finish. Dotted swiss has a woven pattern of dots; stiffening and starch produce organdy.

A MODERN APPROACH TO HEIRLOOM SEWING

A modern zigzag sewing machine with settings to adjust the upper-thread tension and stitch length enable any moderately skilled home sewer to imitate, after just a few hours of practice, fine hand-sewing techniques that formerly took years to learn and weeks for even the most accomplished needlewomen to work. If you don't have a zigzag machine you won't be able to roll and whip a hem, but you can try everything else.

Since children's clothes require so little yardage, even the finest fabrics are relatively within reach. The children will enjoy wearing them as much as you will enjoy sewing with them.

TECHNIQUES

1. Tiny French Seams. Tiny French seams are just like regular French seams except that the enclosed seam allowance is only 1/16".

STEP ONE. No matter what the given seam allowance of the pattern may be, sew the preliminary seam with wrong sides together, 1/8" inside the designated seam line. Press the seam open with both allowances to one side. Trim them to 1/6".

STEP TWO. Using the preliminary seam as a fold guide, realign the pieces with right sides together and stitch the final seam along the original seam line, enclosing the raw edges and leaving a finished seam allowance of 1/8".

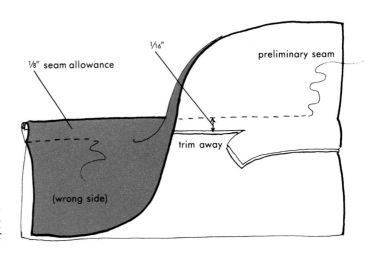

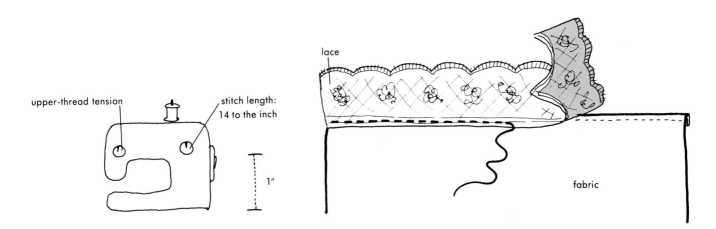

2. Invisible Topstitching. Use this technique when you want to appliqué strips of lace or eyelet.

Shorten the stitch length by increasing the number of stitches per inch to 12 or 14. Loosen the upper-thread tension to almost nothing so that it resembles the tension of very fine hand sewing.

Simply lay the trim on top of the area to be trimmed and topstitch it in place. Basting is perfectly acceptable if it makes you feel more secure, but it is usually unnecessary as the finished edge or seamline you are trimming helps to guide your eye.

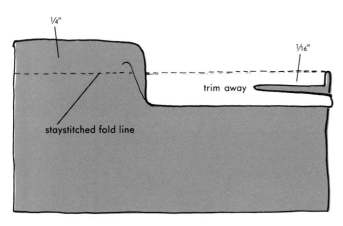

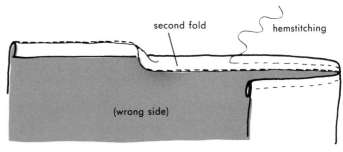

3. Tiny Topstitched Hem.

This hem, also known as the shirt-tail hem, is fun to do once you get the knack. It, too, relies on preparation to control the final detailing.

Staystitch a fold line ¼″ inside the unfinished edge of the hem and press it to the inside. Trim the hem allowance to ¹⁄₁₆″ without cutting off the thread ends at the end of the staystitching (you will need them to get a grip on the cloth to turn the final hem). Grasping the thread ends in one hand, pull with the other to create a slight tension along the staystitched fold line.

Turn a second fold to the inside, this time using the trimmed edge as a fold guide. The tension along the staystitching supports the first fold and keeps the narrow hem allowance from rolling to the outside as you stitch. Topstitch the hem from the inside, leaving the needle in the *down* position to secure the fabric every time you have to reposition your hands.

4. Machine-Rolled and-Whipped Hem.

Once again, the secret is planning ahead with staystitching. Using the same machine settings as before and working from the right side, staystitch a guideline ¼″ inside the raw edge. Trim the hem allowance as close as you dare to the staystitching—¹⁄₁₆″ is nice if you can manage it, ⅛″ will be fine. Set the zigzag width to medium, the stitch length to 16 to 18 per inch, and stitch the hem so that the needle goes over the raw edge when it *zigs* and penetrates the fabric slightly to the left of the guideline when it *zags*.

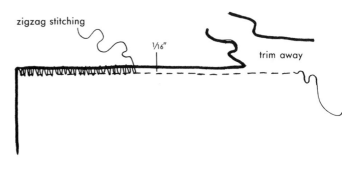

5. Adding Lace to a Rolled-and-Whipped Hem.

Place the lace right side down over the staystitching and catch the edge as you stitch the hem. Press open the tiny seam with the seam allowance facing away from the lace.

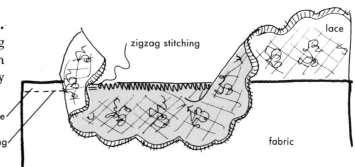

Party Bloomers

Party Bloomers

Although these little bloomers have the look of luxury, they are actually one of the easiest projects in the book, requiring at most two hours of pleasant sewing.

Trimmed here with inch-wide, pure-cotton lace edging and garnished with little satin bows held in place by French knots, they illustrate the machine-rolling and -whipping technique.

You can vary the color of the bows and the French knots for seasonal gifts or substitute anything that strikes your fancy or your budget in place of the French lace. You might even trim away the ruffle allowance at the bottom of the pattern and plan a casing at the elastic line to sew matching bloomers for your next dress project.

Materials

¾ yard of 45″-wide fine cotton batiste, double the length of the bloomer pattern

1½″-wide lace edging double the S–S² distance

Elastic: ⅜″-wide: equal to child's waist measurement

¼″-wide: double child's upper-leg measurement

½ yard of ¼″-wide, double-faced satin ribbon

Six-strand cotton embroidery floss: A few strands of pale blue

Two-ply lingerie thread

The Grid

(If unfamiliar with the grid technique see page 180, or substitute any commercial pattern with an elasticized waist and leg ruffle.)

Fold the appropriate grid and trace the bloomer pattern point-for-point and square-for-square, including the three shaded squares between center front and center back for extra fullness and the one-and-one-half-square depth extension for "bloom."

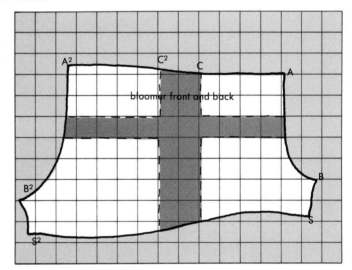

Layout and Cutting

Place the pattern on the folded fabric, matching the vertical grain line to the lengthwise grain of the fabric, and cut out the bloomers.

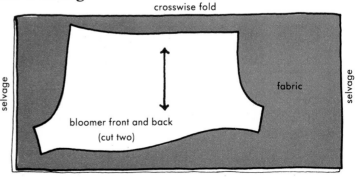

Sewing the Bloomers

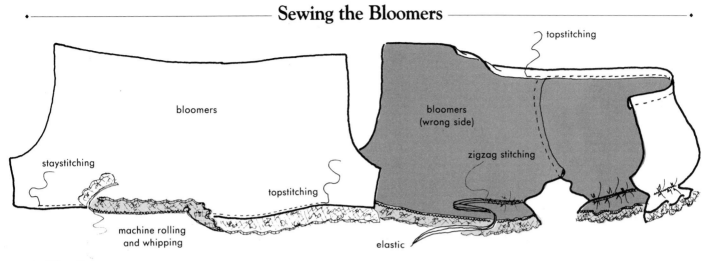

1. The Legs.

THE LACE. Cut a length of the lace edging to match the bottom edge of each leg and use the machine-whipping and -rolling technique to sew it to the bloomers.

THE ELASTIC. Mark the elastic stitching line on the inside of the bloomers one and one half squares above the finished edge.

Cut a length of the ¼" elastic to equal the child's leg measurement and stitch it to the line with a wide zigzag stitch, stretching the elastic evenly throughout the stitching.

2. The Waist. Join the center fronts with a tiny French seam. Turn under ¼" at the top of the bloomers, then fold and topstitch the ¾" casing to the inside.

Cut a length of ⅜" elastic to equal the child's waist measurement. Pin large safety pins crosswise to both ends of the elastic and thread the elastic through the casing. (The crosswise safety pins prevent the other end of the elastic from entering the casing.)

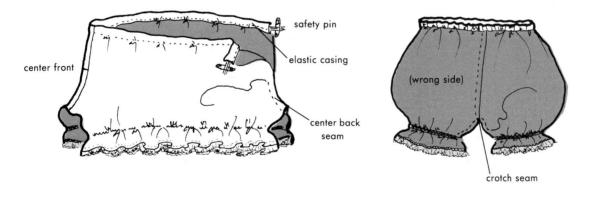

3. Finishing the Bloomers. Join the center back and crotch seams with tiny French seams. Turn the bloomers right side out, pre-tie ribbon bows of whatever size you prefer and tack them to the elastic at the side of each leg with a cluster of French knots.

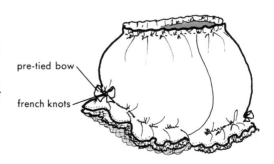

Ruffled Petticoat

Petticoats, in general, are as practical as they are pretty and this confection is no exception.

The simple A-line shape is as suitable for teenagers as it is for little girls. The panels avoid bulky gathers at the waist, yet flare to becoming fullness at the hem, which is enhanced by the sweet, eyelet ruffle. Luxurious ribbon-filled beading covers the seam.

Since sewing this petticoat is a breeze (all three panels are cut from the same pattern and the elastic casing at the waist eliminates the need for a waistband), the real fun is the combination of several different trims for the look of luxury but not necessarily the expense. The yardages are so minimal that you might even consider experimenting with the finest Swiss or French laces and embroideries.

Plan the length so the ruffle peeps out about an inch under the hem of the skirt that will be worn over it.

Materials [for size 5]

44–45″ wide batiste, length of petticoat pattern

Embroidered eyelet edging: 4″ wide [measured at the narrowest part of the scallop] four times the bottom circumference of pattern

1¼″ wide eyelet beading to equal the bottom circumference of pattern

¾ yard of ⅜″-wide elastic for the waist

Double-faced satin ribbon to fit the beading

Two-ply lingerie thread

(See mail-order sources for ordering fine fabrics and eyelets)

The Grid

(If unfamiliar with the grid technique see page 180, or substitute any commercial petticoat pattern with an elasticized waist and hem ruffle.)

Fold the appropriate grid and trace the outline of the pattern point-for-point and square-for-square, noticing the one-square shaded area on each side which creates the A shape, and the one-square casing allowance at the top.

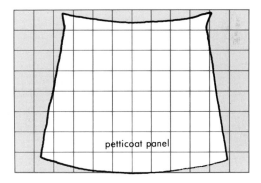

petticoat panel

Layout and Cutting

Fold the fabric vertically in three sections (like a business letter). Place the panel pattern on the top layer with the center aligned along the lengthwise grain and cut out all three panels at once.

lengthwise fold

petticoat (cut three)

lengthwise fold

fabric

Sewing the Petticoat

1. Preparation. The petticoat is completely assembled before the center back seam is joined, which allows you the convenience of working on a flat surface instead of within a cylinder. Also, the raw ends of the elastic, eyelet, ribbon, and beading are all hidden in the final seam allowance. Unorthodox, but speedy.

JOINING THE PANELS. Join the center panel to the left and right side panels with tiny French seams. Leave the center back seam open. Press the final seam allowances away from the center.

THE CASING. Fold the casing allowance to the inside,

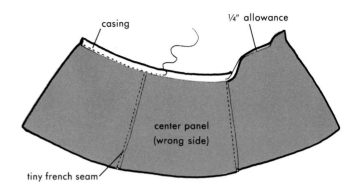

turn up a ¼″ seam allowance and topstitch the casing to the inside, ½″ away from the fold.

2. The Eyelet Ruffle.

THE GATHERING. Cut a length of eyelet edging one and one half times as long as the bottom edge of the petticoat. Install two rows of fine machine gathering ⅛″ apart, starting ⅜″ away from the upper edge of the eyelet. Pull up the gathers to fit the bottom of the petticoat, stroking them with the blunt end of a seam ripper so that they are spread evenly throughout.

JOINING THE RUFFLE. Sew the ruffle to the bottom of the petticoat, with raw edges aligned and wrong sides together, as if you were sewing the preliminary seam of a French seam. Press the seam allowance upward over the right side of the petticoat.

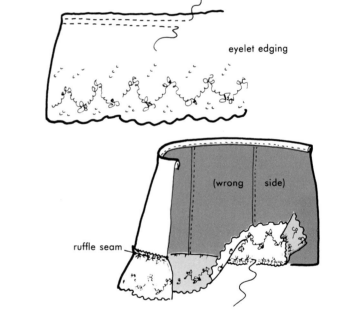

THE BEADING. Thread the ribbon through the beading before pinning and basting it right side up to the right side of the petticoat so that it covers the ruffle seam. Topstitch one side of the beading to the ruffle as close to the seam as possible, the other side to the petticoat.

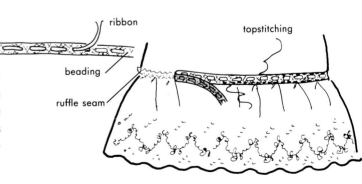

3. Finishing the Petticoat.

THE ELASTIC. Cut a length of elastic to equal the child's waist measurement. Fasten a large safety pin to one end of the elastic and thread it through the casing. Keep the other end of the elastic from disappearing into the casing by fastening another large safety pin through it, too.

THE FINAL SEAM. Close the center back seam with a tiny French seam.

THE BOW. Garnish the bottom of the left side seam with a small ribbon bow tacked to the beading.

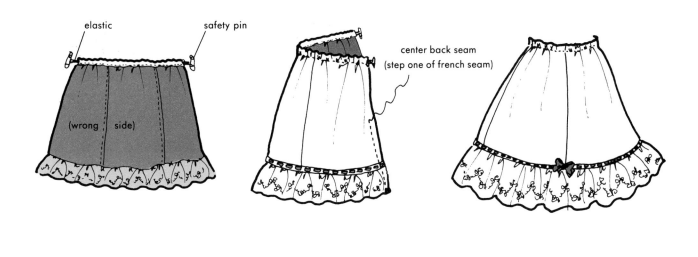

THE STRAPS. If desired (as in cases where there isn't much of a waistline), sew small transparent plastic buttons to the inside of the casing approximately 2″ away from each side of the center front and center back.

Cut lengths of ¾″ cotton-twill tape to serve as shoulder straps, measuring the length from the buttons in the back, up over the shoulder, to the buttons in the front, planning to cross the straps over each other and adding as much growth allowance as you like.

Machine hem the ends of the straps, sew buttonholes in both ends, and button the straps to the inside of the waistband.

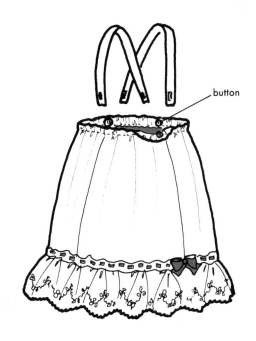

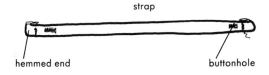

Princess Slip

Slips stop itchy fabrics from chafing tender skin, give skirts extra body, keep synthetic fabrics from clinging to tights, and add to the air of femininity and the excitement of dressing up. Here, two coordinated edgings illustrate how one technique can be adapted in an infinite variety of combinations.

The princess silhouette has shaped seams that follow the contour of the body and create a smooth-fitting center panel. The panel seams may be flared to add fullness to the bottom of skirt without bulk at the waist, the side panel eliminates the need for underarm seams and makes a smoother line under the side seams of the dress, and the cut on the straight grain at the side helps prevent twisting.

In a pinch on a rainy afternoon, a colorful sash added and the slip can become a ballet costume. Nothing is wrong with making the Princess Slip and Party Bloomers out of matching fabric for a summer sundress, either!

The order of construction is carefully planned so you will be able to work on the flat as you trim the slip and enclose all the raw edges of the eyelet in the tiny French seams.

If your child dislikes putting things on over her head, you can hem the raw edges of front and back at the shoulders, omit the seam, and substitute a button-and-loop closing.

Materials

¾ yard white batiste, lawn, or percale (100% cotton recommended)

1½ yards of ¼"-wide scalloped eyelet edging for neckline trim

1½ yards of ½"-wide scalloped eyelet edging for hem trim

A scrap of ¼"-wide, double-faced, satin ribbon for neckline bow

The Grids

(If unfamiliar with the grid technique see page 180, or substitute any commercial slip pattern.)

The Princess Slip has several subtle changes at the neck and armhole which make the pattern more complicated than it looks. This need not alarm you, however, because adding or removing as little as ⅛" from each side of each princess seam will increase or decrease the total girth by 1" and handily solve most fitting problems.

Fold the appropriate grid and trace the slip pattern point-for-point and square-for-square, adjusting the princess seams and A–H lines according to the changes you made in the basic sloper.

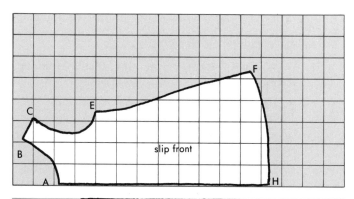

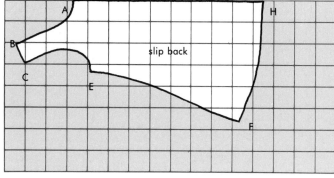

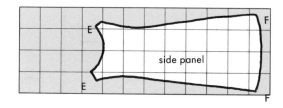

Layout and Cutting

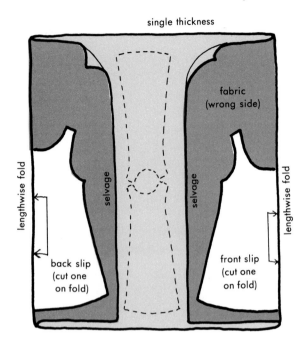

single thickness

fabric
(wrong side)

lengthwise fold

selvage

back slip
(cut one
on fold)

selvage

front slip
(cut one
on fold)

lengthwise fold

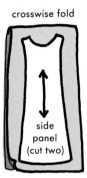

crosswise fold

side
panel
(cut two)

Gate fold the fabric so that you can place the center front and back of the patterns along the folds, as shown. When you have cut out the front and back pieces, refold the fabric in the center, place the side panel pattern over the folded fabric, and cut out two side panels.

Sewing the Slip

1. The Neck and Armholes.

THE SHOULDER SEAM. Close one of the shoulder seams with a tiny French seam and press carefully.

THE NECK. Measure the neckline opening and cut a length of the eyelet to fit. Machine whip and roll the eyelet to the slip following the technique on page 78, taking care to ease the eyelet around the curve so that it won't distort the shape of the neckline. Press the tiny seam down and edgestitch the slip over it from the outside, if necessary.

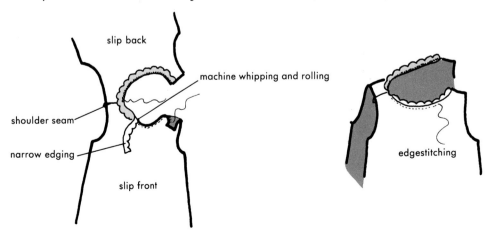

slip back

machine whipping and rolling

shoulder seam

narrow edging

slip front

edgestitching

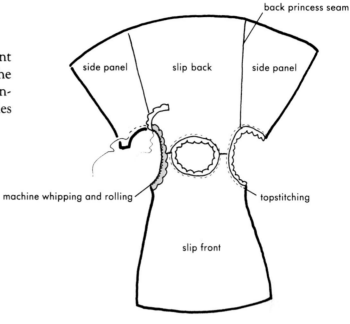

THE ARMHOLES. Join the two side panels to the front with French seams at the princess seams, and close the remaining shoulder seam. Measure the armhole openings, cut the lengths of eyelet, and finish the armholes as you did the neck.

2. Finishing the Slip. Close one of the remaining princess seams in the back with a narrow French seam, and trim the bottom of the slip as you did the neck and armhole, this time with the wider eyelet edging.

Complete the slip by closing the final princess seam in the back. Tie and tack the little ribbon bow to the center of the front neckline with French knots.

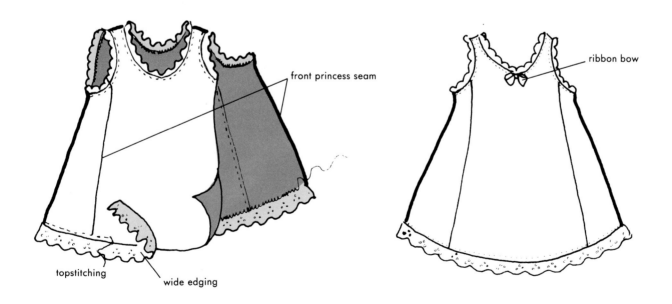

Active Play

artoonists draw "action lines" streaming behind a figure to indicate speed. Sportswear designers put speed stripes on the clothing itself. Striped panels circle wrists, biceps, chest: appliquéd stripes run over sleeves, down legs, across shoulders. Striped fabrics are multicolored, diagonal, horizontal, vertical, contrasting.

In fact, fabric is the real story of active sportswear. Behind the fabrics are the fibers and the looms. In the beginning there were natural fibers: silk, cotton, wool, linen. Silk and wool are animal fibers; cotton and linen are plant fibers. All must be cultivated, gathered, purified, spun into thread, and bleached before dyeing and weaving. Of the four, only expensive silk can accept brilliantly colored dyes.

Today's synthetic fibers have a petroleum base, are "brewed" rather than spun, and produce colorless filaments rather than twisted threads. Stretch and strength can be added to the brew and the width of the resulting continuous filament is designed to withstand the pressures of modern knitting looms. Although the filaments cannot be penetrated by water (the underlying secret of wash-and-wear) they can accept brilliant modern dyes. Thus bright colors, once the privilege of royalty, have blossomed everywhere.

Although most children belong to the "If it's bright, it's swell" club, adults are conditioned to turn green with envy, feel blue, hate yellow cowards, and tradition has it that brides wear white, baby girls wear pink, boys wear blue, and scarlet women mean big trouble. Now babies wear orange and men, once slaves to navy and gray, sport rugby shirts with turquoise and scarlet stripes. Color has come to symbolize strength and affluence and a nation on the move into the next century.

Thomas Eakins's portrait of a baby at play in 1876 captures the intense concentration of childhood. The horse and buggy lie temporarily forgotten in favor of the special fascination of the alphabet blocks. Although the style of the play dress is outmoded, every child's wardrobe still includes at least one pair of striped socks.

TECHNIQUES

Sewing Knit Fabrics

All stretch fabrics are a knit of some type. For some reason, many people are slightly in awe of them and hesitate to work with them. But in reality knits are so forgiving of minor errors that they are as easy to sew as they are comfortable to wear. Knits are quick. Basting is seldom necessary and careful finishing techniques can be forgotten. Wristbands, anklebands, waistbands, crewnecks, and turtlenecks are easily improvised from self-fabric, taking advantage of the stretch of the crossgrain. Since the cut edges of knits don't fray, seam allowances usually can be left untreated.

The first knitting loom was a ribbed frame for silk stockings built in Scotland by Jedediah Strutt in 1758. Nowadays, you name it and we knit it. The type of knit, fiber content, and thickness influence fabric performance. If the edges curl when it is cut, it is a jersey or single knit; if it lies flat, it is a double or rib knit. Stretch a cut edge of the fabric to determine the direction of the knit. Runs will develop in the top edge and the bottom will remain unchanged, just as in home knitting.

Some knits have a pile similar to woven fabrics. Velour is velvet with a knit rather than woven background. Stretch terry has cotton loops that are unclipped; stretch fleece has a thick, cushiony pile. Lycra and spandex, used for bathing suits in children's wear, have elastic in the fiber which gives it a two-way stretch, a desirable attribute formerly confined to sturdy ladies' underpinnings.

Sewing equipment also influences fabric performance. Ballpoint needles are a must and strong thread, such as polyester or cotton wrapped polyester core are recommended. If you have state-of-the-art equipment, your machine probably has special disks or dials built in for knit seams, seam finishes, and buttonholes. You may even have an overlocker which uses three spools of thread simultaneously and cuts away the excess seam allowance as it overcasts the edge of the seam. Don't worry if you don't have state-of-the-art equipment, however. A good, basic, zigzag machine can do a very nice job with manually set controls, but even if your machine does only straight seaming, do not despair. Knits will still be easy for you to sew if you understand the effect you are aiming to imitate and the property of the particular knit.

1. The Seams.

STITCHING. The idea is to provide for stretch and recovery. Stitches must withstand the pull of action without breaking or forcing the knit out of shape.

Some machines have a special knit setting that goes back and forth several times over each stitch, others form a serpentine pattern. Follow the manufacturer's directions and experiment with your fabric until you reach a good norm. If your machine is only capable of a few basic zigzag stitches, use a very narrow zigzag setting and short stitch length.

Straight stitching machines may require some experimentation. The idea is to get the stitches to nestle into the knit. Try a short stitch, say 14 to 16 per inch, and if your machine permits, loosen the upper-thread tension. After stitching, tug on the seam to see if the thread holds. Some people like to pull the knit slightly as they stitch while others find that this stretches the knit out of shape permanently. Experiment to find the ideal combination for your stitching style and fabric.

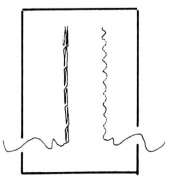

automatic stitch settings

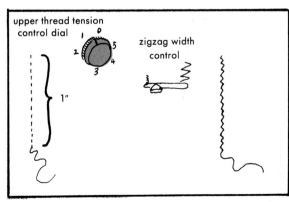

straight stitches   narrow zigzag stitches

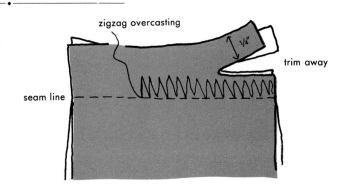

FINISHING. If you do a great deal of sewing, the special overcasting feature will be a great boon to you. If not, imitate the effect as follows: loosen the upper-thread tension, if possible; keep the stitch length at 14 to 16 per inch, set the zigzag at its widest setting, and overcast both seam allowances simultaneously, stitching ¼″ inside the raw edge. Trim the seam allowance to the points of the overcasting as a final step. Remember, in many cases, knit seams do not have to be finished at all. Once again, . . . experiment.

2. Stretch Buttonholes. The flexibility that makes stretch fabrics so desirable for active wear can be a drawback occasionally, especially concerning buttonholes.

The buttonholes must be sturdy yet flexible. If the fabric is reinforced with interfacing or bonding for stability, then the stretch property is lost and the buttonhole will have a tendency to gap. If the flexibility is kept, the buttonhole may look ragged and poorly finished. Also, each knit fabric has its own stretch properties and what might be right for one knit is not necessarily the answer for another.

Always machine test a scrap of your fabric until you are satisfied with the results. Many modern machines have a special knit buttonhole setting or technique. Follow it if you like the results. If not, or your machine doesn't have a specific knit buttonhole, you have several choices:

THE FLEXIBLE BUTTONHOLE. The first step may remind you of the good old-fashioned buttonhole. Out-line the buttonhole with machine staystitching, setting the stitch length as short as is practical (a good average is 16 stitches per inch) and setting as light an upper-thread tension as your machine will produce. Sew down one side. Leaving the point of the needle in the fabric, raise the presser foot and pivot 90 degrees. Take three or four stitches across the short end. Pivot again and finish the outline.

When you arrive back at the starting point, set the machine to a narrow zigzag that approximates half the buttonhole width and zigzag down the first side of the buttonhole. Widen the setting and bar tack the end with a few stitches set at zero stitch length. Turn the buttonhole, zigzag down the other side and finish with another bar tack.

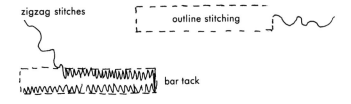

THE STABILIZED BUTTONHOLE. The front openings of knit sweaters are faced and stabilized with grosgrain ribbon. You may use ribbon, twill tape, strips of press-on interfacing, or self-facing bonded into position with fusible webbing.

Ribbon and tape are suitable for narrow facings because of their pre-set widths. Ribbon offers a wider choice of color; tape is sportier. Iron-on interfacing and fusible bonding offer a greater choice of widths and more control over fraying, but the heat of the iron can mat some fabrics.

In any case, a faced or interfaced knit behaves much more like a woven fabric, and you should now be able to proceed with whatever buttonhole method is customary for you. Let your fabric and your machine's capabilities be your guide.

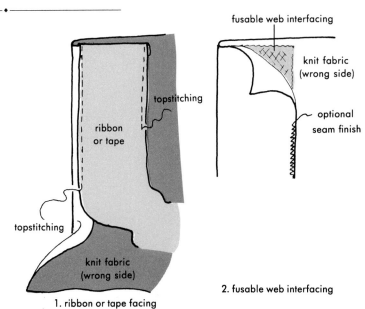

Stretch Bathing Suit

The stripes on the illustrated suit are printed on the bias; the suit is actually cut on the straight lengthwise grain.

No matter if the stripes are horizontal or vertical or bias. All you need is a nice round tummy to fill out the suit to remind you of the way the wind fills out the colorful sails of a magnificent yacht.

You don't even have to stick to stripes. Mix and match a few remnants from the sale table, cut them all out at the same time, sew them assembly-line style, and you'll have an impressive beach or pool wardrobe in an hour or so.

If your little boy feels left out, read the drawstring instructions for the jogging pants in this chapter, trace the lower half of the pattern, and soon he will be all set with his own wardrobe of trunks.

Materials

Spandex or lycra fabric: main color one length equal to 14 squares of your grid

¼ yard of contrast color

The Grids

(If unfamiliar with the grid technique see page 180, or substitute any commercial bathing suit pattern designed for stretch fabrics.)

Fold the appropriate grids and trace the front, the back, and the crotch lining patterns point-for-point and square-for-square.

Since the neck and armhole cutouts are already enlarged and the pattern is intended for fabrics with maximum stretch properties, you can probably safely subscribe to the theory that "if it ain't broke, don't fix it," and cut the pattern as is, without alterations. If absolutely necessary, however, transfer any changes you have made to the A–H line of the front and back. Further changes can be made at shoulders and side seams as indicated by the shaded areas.

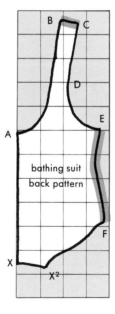

bathing suit
back pattern

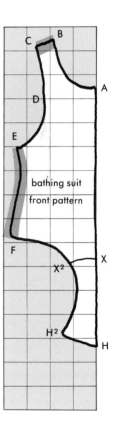

bathing suit
front pattern

Layout and Cutting

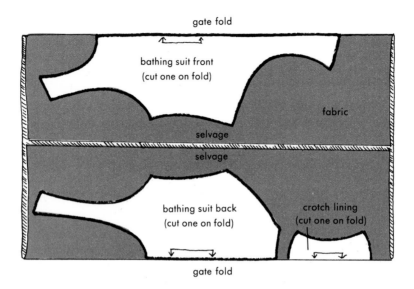

gate fold

bathing suit front
(cut one on fold)

fabric

selvage

selvage

bathing suit back
(cut one on fold)

crotch lining
(cut one on fold)

gate fold

Gate fold the fabric so that the selvages meet in the center and cut all the pattern pieces on a lengthwise fold according to the general principle of the illustrated layout.

Sewing the Bathing Suit

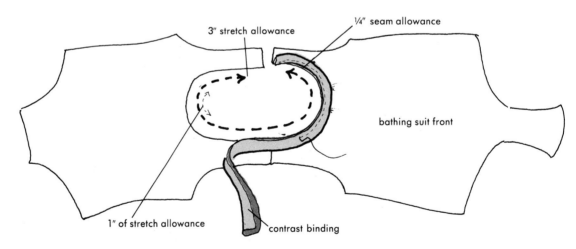

3" stretch allowance

¼" seam allowance

bathing suit front

1" of stretch allowance

contrast binding

1. The Neck Opening.

MEASURING THE BINDING. Close one of the shoulder seams and measure the circumference of the neck seam between the back and front edges of the remaining open shoulder.

CUTTING THE BINDING. Cut the binding strip on the cross-grain of the contrast fabric 1½" wide and 3" shorter than the neck seam measurement.

SEWING THE BINDING. Fold the binding in half lengthwise, wrong sides together. Stretch seam it to the right side of the bathing suit, matching all the cut edges at the shoulder seams and around the neck. Approximately 1" of the stretch allowance should be concentrated in the scoop at the bottom of the back cutout, the rest should be evenly distributed throughout.

Turn the neck binding seam allowance to the inside and close the remaining shoulder seam.

2. The Armholes. Similarly bind the armholes, subtracting a 2″ stretch allowance from the armhole measurement. Once again, turn the seam allowance to the inside before closing the side seams.

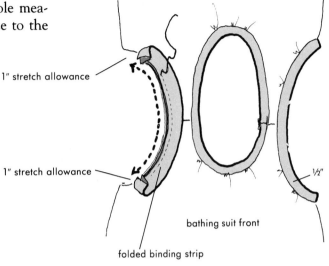

1″ stretch allowance

1″ stretch allowance

½″

bathing suit front

folded binding strip

3. Finishing the Bathing Suit.

THE CROTCH LINING. Baste the crotch lining piece to the inside of the suit, wrong sides together, and raw edges matching at the leg edges and back crotch seam.

BINDING THE LEG. Measure and cut leg bindings as you did before, subtracting 3″ from the circumference of the leg seam for the stretch allowance.

Bind the leg as you did the neck and the armhole, securing the sides of the crotch lining in the stitching.

Turn the leg binding seam allowance to the inside and close the crotch seam to finish the suit.

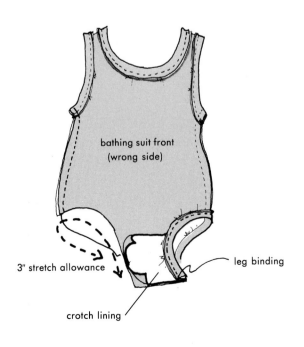

bathing suit front
(wrong side)

3″ stretch allowance

leg binding

crotch lining

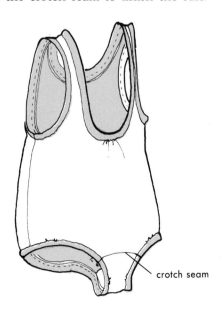

crotch seam

Hooded Beach Jacket

The hooded jacket is a staple of the modern child's wardrobe.

The hood will come in handy when a child's hair is wet after swimming if the jacket is made to coordinate with the bathing suit, as shown; or a sweat-shirt fabric or velour can be chosen to coordinate with the pants if you plan a jogging or warm-up suit.

Materials

50"–60" wide stretch terry, velour, or sweat shirt fabric: center back length plus 6"

¼ yard of contrast stretch fabric for wrist- and facebands

Snap tape equal to center front length plus 3"

Upholstery cord for drawstring equal to circumference of hood opening plus 1 yard

The Grids

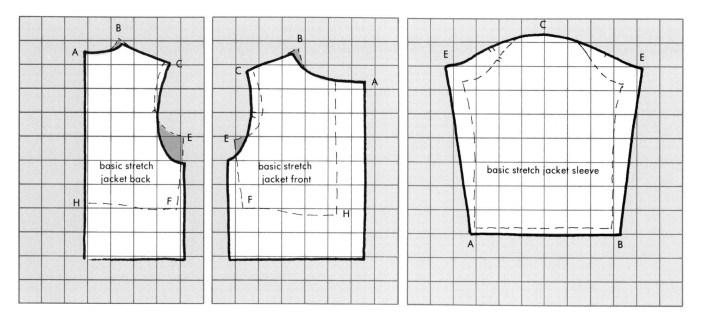

(If unfamiliar with the grid technique, see page 180, or substitute any commercial hooded-jacket pattern designed for stretch fabrics.)

Fold the appropriate grids and trace the basic stretch jacket sloper pattern, noticing the shaded areas where the armhole has been lowered and the side seam extended from the original basic slopers to provide the extra ease necessary for outerwear.

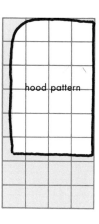

Layout and Cutting

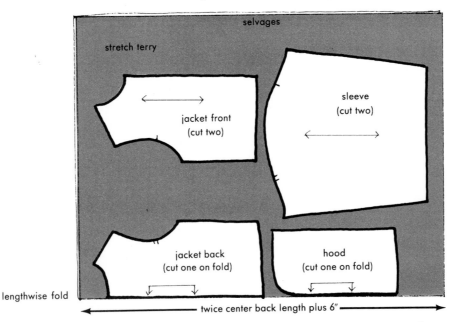

Fold the fabric in half lengthwise, wrong sides together to prevent the pile from snagging itself, and lay out the pattern pieces according to the general princi- ples of the sample layout, being sure to align the arrows with the lengthwise grain and placing all fold symbols against the lengthwise fold.

Sewing the Jacket

1. The Shoulders. Join the fronts to the backs at the shoulders, finishing these and all other seams as in- structed in the "Techniques" section of this chapter. If your terry is very stretchy, add a layer of seam tape to the seam.

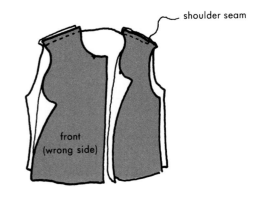

2. The Sleeves.

THE WRISTBANDS. The finished width of the wrist- band will be governed by the width of the stripes in your fabric, but should approximate 1½". Double the desired width and cut a length of contrast trim on the horizontal grain to fit comfortably over the child's hand when stretched, remembering to add ⅝" seam allow- ance on all sides. Fold the wristband in half, wrong sides together, and stretch seam it to the bottom of the sleeve.

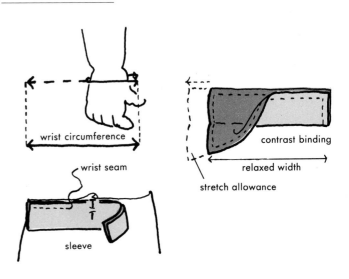

THE ARMHOLE, UNDERARM, SIDE, AND WRIST-BAND SEAMS. Pin and stitch the sleeve into the armhole before closing the side, underarm, and wristband seams in one continuous seam.

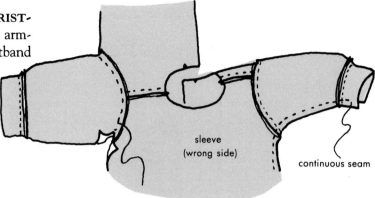

3. The Waistband. Subtract 3″ from the bottom circumference of the jacket and cut a 4½″ wide waistband on the crosswise grain of the self-fabric. Fold the band in half lengthwise, wrong sides together, and stretch seam it to the bottom of the jacket.

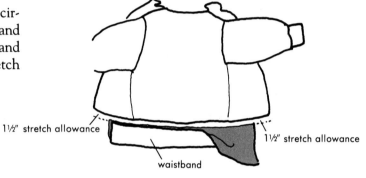

4. The Front Closing.

THE RIGHT FRONT. Overcast raw edge at the center front, from the bottom of the waistband to the top of the neck. Cut a length of snap tape to fit the total center front measurement plus a ½″ hem allowance at top and bottom.

Turn the allowances under and lay the prong half of the snap tape right side up over the right side of the jacket. Topstitch the left edge of the tape ¼″ inside the center front turnback line, fold everything to the inside, and topstitch the remaining free edge of the tape to the jacket.

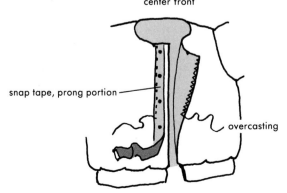

THE LEFT FRONT. Similarly overcast the raw edges at center front. Fold the turnback to the inside, pin the socket half of the tape to the right side of the jacket, and topstitch both sides through all layers.

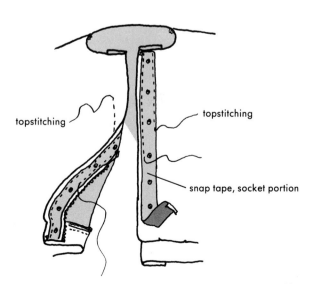

101

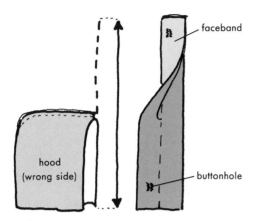

faceband

hood
(wrong side)

buttonhole

5. The Hood.

THE TOP SEAM. Fold the hood in half lengthwise, right sides together. Stitch the seam from front to back ¼″ away from the raw edge, tapering the seam allowance to nothing as you finish rounding the curve.

THE FACEBAND. The finished width of the band looks better if it is narrower than the wristband, ideally not exceeding 1″ in width. Fold the hood in half lengthwise, right sides together. Close and finish the top seam of the hood. Cut the contrast trim to fit the exact measurement of the front edge of the hood, once again centering the stripes attractively before doubling the finished width and adding seam allowance.

THE DRAWSTRING OPENING. Work a ¾″-long, special knit technique buttonhole centered 1″ above the neck seam at either end of the turnback half of the strip. Fold the strip in half lengthwise, right sides together, and seam it to the front of the hood so that the drawstring openings are on the inside.

Finishing the Jacket.

THE NECK SEAM. Pin the hood to the neck seam, right sides together, matching the fold of the finished faceband to the center turnback fold of the jacket, and seam them together ¼″ from the raw edge.

THE DRAWSTRING. Thread the upholstery cord through the faceband and knot both ends to prevent it from pulling through inadvertently.

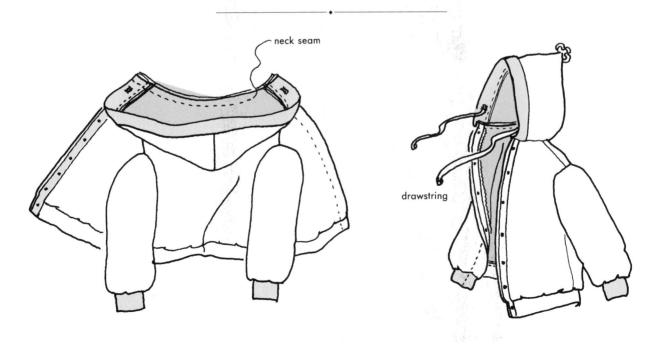

neck seam

drawstring

Boy's Jogging Suit

Boy's Jogging Suit

Girls jog too! Let your color scheme and your child's gender determine the final description of this essentially unisex outfit.

The jacket is cut from the same basic pattern as the Hooded Beach Jacket, except that the collar replaces the hood to finish the neck seam. The action panels are cut from contrast fabric. The piping can be bought or you can custom coordinate your own. Choose velour as illustrated or substitute any other stretch fabric.

Materials

60″ wide stretch velour fabric:

Main color equal to 2½ times the side-seam measurement of the pants

¼ yard of contrast color

One 3-yard package purchased piping or ¼ yard woven fabric for sewn trim

One large-toothed plastic separating zipper approximately 4″ longer than center front jacket measurement

¾″-wide elastic to fit child's back waist measurement

The Grids

(If unfamiliar with the grid technique see page 180, or substitute any commercial pants pattern with drawstring waist for the pants and any jacket pattern with front opening and long sleeves for the jacket.)

THE PANTS. Fold the appropriate grids and trace the pants sloper point-for-point and square-for-square, transferring individualized fitting changes as required. The shaded areas represent a modified crotch curve suitable for stretch fabrics, a 1½″ casing allowance above the waist, and a ½″ additional seam allowance at center front.

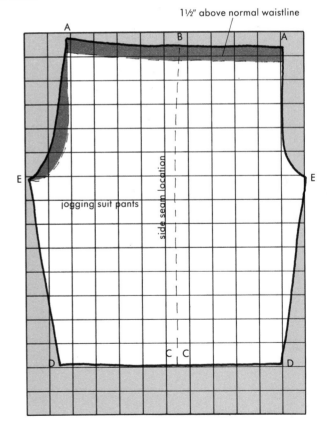

1½″ above normal waistline

side seam location

jogging suit pants

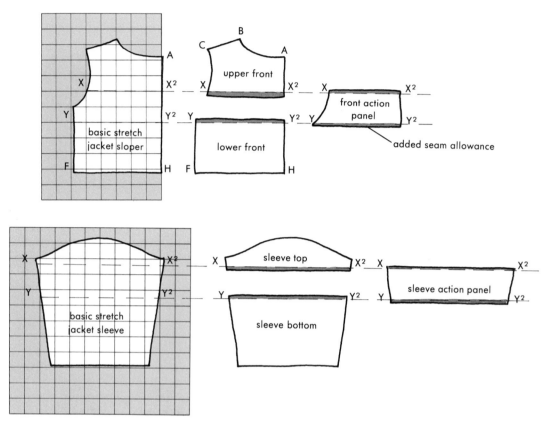

THE JACKET. Fold the appropriate grids and trace the basic bodice and sleeve jacket slopers for the Hooded Beach Jacket. Draft the action panel patterns and the upper and lower front and sleeve sections as the stylelines indicate, remembering to add ⅝" seam allowances as indicated by the shaded areas.

Layout and Cutting

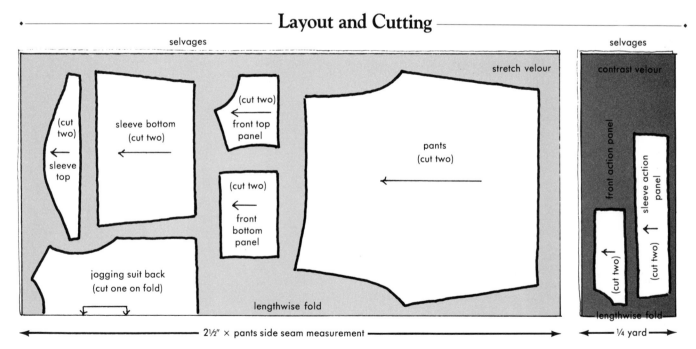

Fold the fabric in half lengthwise, wrong sides together, and lay out the pieces of the suit according to the general principles of the illustration, noticing the one-way layout. Most knits and all velour are napped fabrics and should be cut the same as velvet and corduroy. Choose the direction of the nap for both jacket and contrast panels as described on page 100.

Sewing the Pants

1. The Seams. Join the center back seam, finishing it or not as you prefer. Join the center front seam, leaving a 1″ seam allowance.

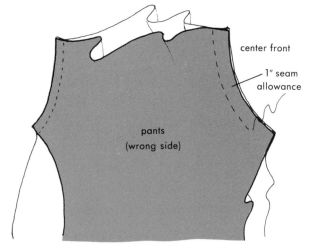

2. The Waistband.

THE DRAWSTRING OPENINGS. When spread open, the wide seam allowance acts as an interfacing to keep the buttonholes for the drawstring openings from sagging. Stitch ⅝″ vertical buttonholes through both the pants and the seam allowance, starting ¼″ below the fold line and ½″ away from the center front seam. Trim the remaining seam allowance to ¼″ starting at the crotch curve and stopping ¼″ below the buttonhole.

THE CASING. Fold the casing allowance to the inside along the fold line, turn up the ½″ seam allowance, and topstitch it to the inside of the waist.

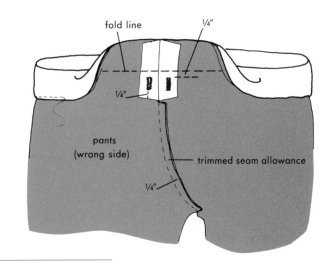

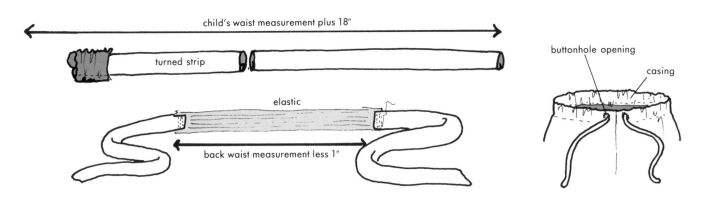

THE DRAWSTRING. Cut a 2″ wide strip on the lengthwise grain to equal the child's waist measurement plus 18″. Seam and turn the strip and cut it in half. Cut a length of ¾″ elastic to equal 1″ less than the child's back waist measurement. Topstitch a tie to each end of the elastic, as shown, and thread the tie through the casing so that the elastic is centered at the center back of the pants. Knot the ends of the ties to prevent raveling.

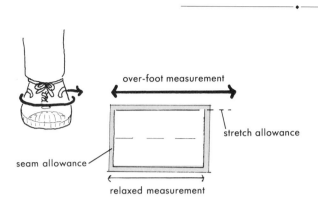

over-foot measurement

stretch allowance

seam allowance

relaxed measurement

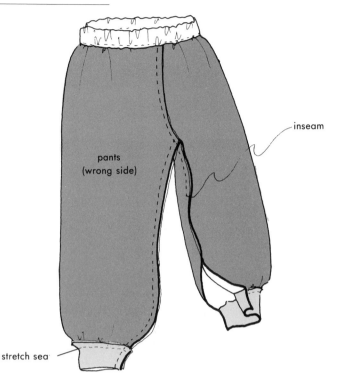

inseam

pants
(wrong side)

stretch sea

3. Finishing the Pants.

THE ANKLEBAND. Gently stretch a horizontal length of contrast velour to comfortably fit the foot circumference. Double the desired depth of the band, add seam allowance all around, and cut the band from the relaxed fabric. Stretch seam it to the bottom of the pants before closing the inseam.

Sewing the Jacket

1. Assembling the Panels.
Baste the piping to the seam lines of all the action panels, reviewing the instructions for piped seams on page 154, if necessary. The piping does not stretch, of course, so be careful not to stretch the knit fabric as you stitch.

Join the upper and lower fronts and sleeves to the appropriate panels using the basting stitches as a seam guide, again taking care not to stretch your knit out of shape as you work.

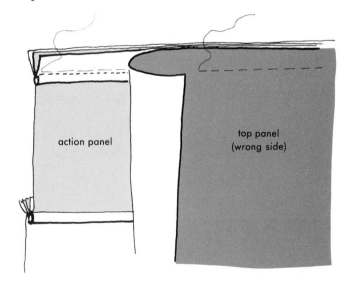

action panel

top panel
(wrong side)

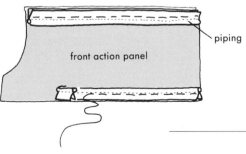

front action panel

piping

2. The Seaming.
Plan a 2½"-deep stretch cuff and finish the wrist of the sleeve before joining the shoulder, sleeve, underarm, and side seams. (It really is as easy as it sounds; just be sure that the piping and action panels meet at the underarm seam.) Finish the waistband exactly as for the Hooded Beach Jacket on page 101.

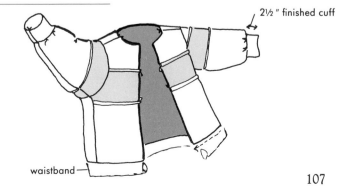

2½" finished cuff

waistband

107

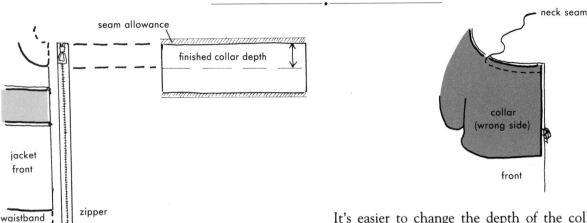

seam allowance

finished collar depth

jacket
front

waistband
depth

zipper

neck seam

collar
(wrong side)

front

3. Finishing the Jacket.

THE COLLAR. Because the stretch qualities of the knit produce a very nice rolled collar from a simple rectangle, the band technique works well at the neckline too. Just measure the circumference of the neck opening and cut a collar to fit exactly, without stretching.

It's easier to change the depth of the collar than the length of the zipper. Compare the zipper to the front opening of the jacket and plan the depth of your collar so that the top fold line will coincide with the top of the zipper stop. Double the measurement and add seam allowance as you would for any stretchband finish.

Cut the collar on the lengthwise grain of the fabric and, with right sides together and raw edges matching at neckline and center front, seam one long edge to the neck.

THE ZIPPER. Separate the halves of the zipper. Baste and stitch them right side down over the right sides of the center front so that the bound edge of the zipper tape covers the raw edges of the jacket, collar, and waistband.

Turn the zipper to the inside. Fold in the remaining raw edges of the collarband and slipstitch them to the zipper tape and the inside of the neck seam.

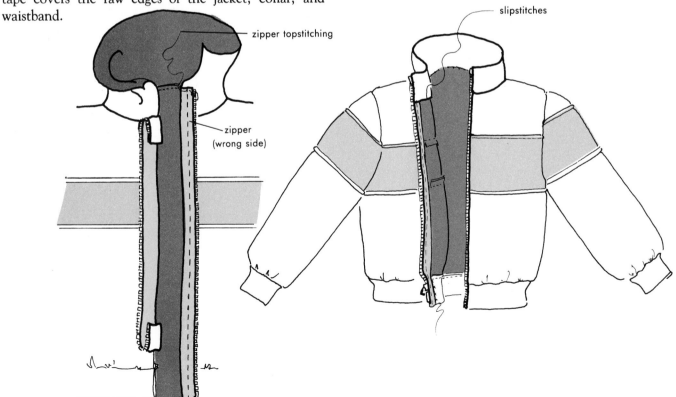

zipper topstitching

zipper
(wrong side)

slipstitches

The Turtleneck Jersey

The Turtleneck Jersey

This versatile jersey pattern is the foundation of endless variations. Make it as is, with long sleeves and turtleneck for winter, or choose short sleeves with a lightweight cotton-knit and borrow the crewneck technique from the Raglan Shirt for summer. You could even try a rugby stripe topped with the full-fashioned collar and placket technique from the Girl's Warm-up Suit . . . in which case it would be fun to embroider your own designer logo in place of the more famous alligator.

Materials

60"-wide stretch jersey fabric, double the overarm sleeve length

¼" yard twill tape

The Grids

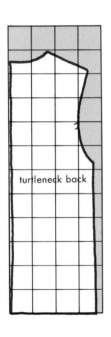
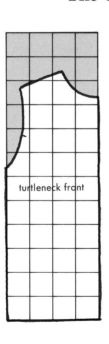
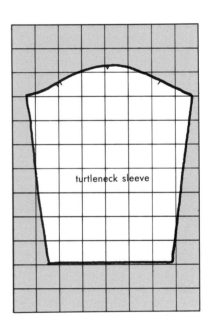

(If unfamiliar with the grid technique see page 180, or substitute any commercial stretch jersey pattern.)

Fold the appropriate grids and trace the bodice and sleeve slopers point-for-point and square-for-square, noticing the shaded areas where the neck and armhole curves have been modified to accommodate stretch fabrics.

Layout and Cutting

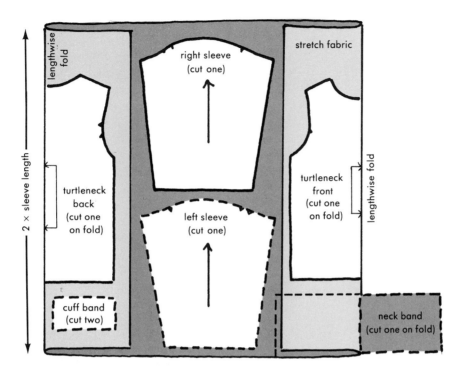

Gate fold the fabric and cut the jersey according to the general principles of the illustrated layout, noticing that center front and center back are on a lengthwise fold.

If your jersey has a stripe, be very sure to match the stripes at the side seams. Match the notch of the sleeve cap to the armhole notch of the front to coordinate a stripe pattern over the sleeves.

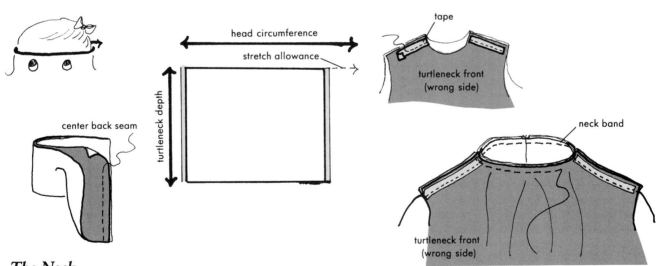

1. The Neck.

MEASURING. Stretch a horizontal length of the jersey to comfortably fit the circumference of the child's head. Mark the measurement, allow the fabric to relax, and cut the neckband to the resulting width and to a depth of six squares.

THE SEAMING. Cut a length of twill tape the same length as the shoulder seam, and stitch it into the seam as you close it to prevent the natural stretch of the fabric from causing the shoulder to sag. Also close the center back of the neckband.

Fold the neckband in half, wrong sides together, and stretch seam it to the right side of the jersey, positioning the band seam at center back.

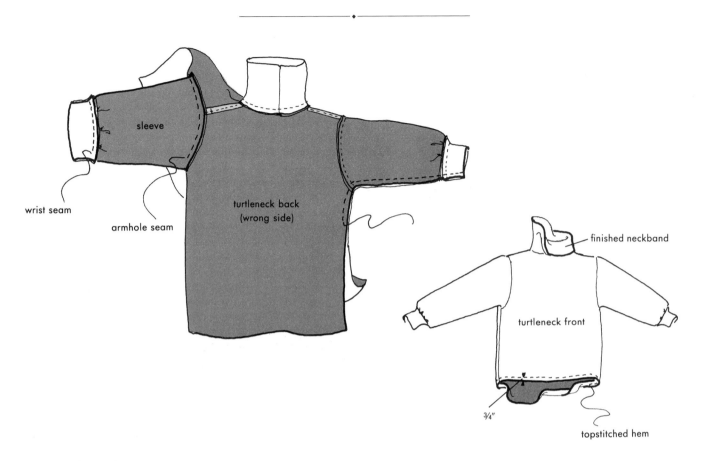

2. Finishing the Jersey.

THE SLEEVE. Prepare a wristband as for the turtleneck on page 111, stretching the fabric to fit over the child's hand, and planning a finished depth of approximately one and one half squares. Stretch seam the wristband to the bottom of the sleeve before setting the sleeve in the armhole.

THE REMAINING SEAMS AND HEM. Close the side, underarm, and wristband seams in one continuous stitching. Finish the bottom of the shirt with a doubled hem topstitched ¾″ above the fold.

Girl's Warm-up Suit

Girl's Warm-up Suit

The girl's jacket has a purchased, full-fashioned collar of the type you find on rugby shirts, and purchased ribbing rather than self-bands at waist, wrist, and ankle.

Ribbing is quite easy to find; the collar may be a little harder. Consult the mail-order sources at the end of the book. Ask for a "full-fashioned child's knit collar" in a choice of small or large. Major manufacturers order thousands at a time and thousands of yards of ribbed trim dyed or knit in the color that the design requires. You will hardly want thousands of collars or yards of ribbing, but there's no reason not to buy white and custom dye it. Test dye a small piece before committing yourself to the color, and never hope to match your base color but, rather, complement it.

Materials

44–45"-wide fleece fabric measuring 2½ times the length of the pants side seam

Full-fashioned ribbed collar

1 yard purchased ribbing, 2" wide

¾"-wide elastic to fit child's back waist measurement

½"-wide twill tape, five times the length of the pants side seam

¼ yard snap tape for neck closing

Fabric dye, if desired

The Grids

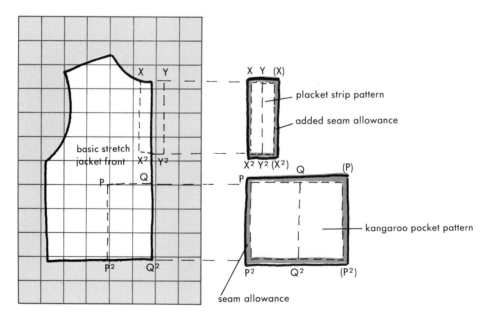

(If unfamiliar with the grid technique see page 180, or substitute any commercial jacket and pants pattern designed for stretch fabrics.)

The basic jacket grid is identical to the Hooded Beach Jacket and the Boy's Jogging Suit. Points $X–X^2–Y–Y^2$ delineate the stylelines for the front placket strip. Points $P–P^2–Q–Q^2$ outline the stylelines of the kangaroo-pocket rectangle.

Trace the finished placket pattern and add ¼" seam allowance outside points $X–X^2–Y^2–X^2–X$, as shown. Similarly add ¼" seam allowance outside points $P^2–P–Q–P–P^2$ to complete the pocket pattern.

The pants pattern is identical to that for the jogging suit.

Layout and Cutting

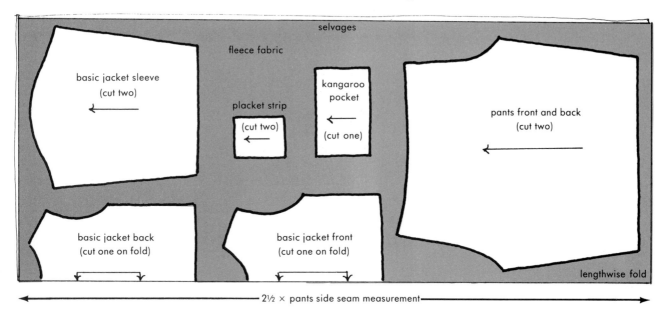

Follow the general principles of the basic layout, being sure to place both front and back jacket patterns on the lengthwise fold of the fabric.

Sewing the Jacket

Follow the general directions for the Hooded Beach Jacket and Jogging Jacket with the following exceptions:

1. The Placket Closing.

THE SNAP TAPE. Mark the center of the right half of each placket strip with a faint pencil mark midway be-

tween the fold line and the seam line on the right side.

Separate the halves of the snap tape, and center each portion right side up over the marking. Topstitch the tape to the placket, placing the first snap (and matching socket) at least ¼" below the neck seam line.

Fold the prepared strips in half lengthwise, right sides together, and seam the top of the placket closed. Trim the corners and turn the plackets right side out.

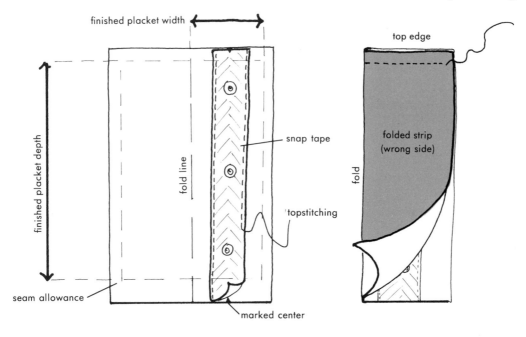

STITCHING THE PLACKET. Topstitch the outline of the placket styleline X–X^2–Y^2–Y on the right side of the jacket.

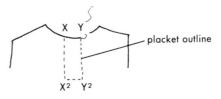

warm-up suit front

Stitch one of the strips wrong side down over the right side of the outline, seam lines flush with the staystitching and the finished edge of the top flush with the neck seam line. (Note that the neck seam allowance of the jacket extends beyond the top of the placket. Note also that the seam allowance at the bottom of the placket strip extends below the staystitching at the bottom of the outline.)

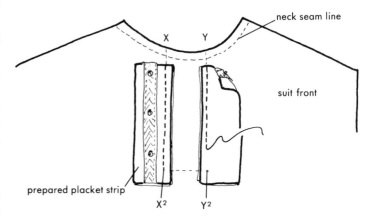

Stitch the placket to the jacket between the neck seam line and the bottom of the outline. Similarly stitch the remaining portion of the placket to the left side of the outline, socket side up. (When both strips are in place, you may be reminded of a window with open shutters.)

SECURING THE PLACKET ON THE INSIDE. Slash the center of the jacket in an upside down Y shape within the stitched outline, as shown.

Use the staystitched line X^2–Y^2–X^2 at the bottom as a guideline to fold the triangle of the Y cutout to the inside. Turn the placket strips to the inside also.

Overlap the bottoms of the placket strips and stitch them to the triangle, once again using the staystitching as a guide.

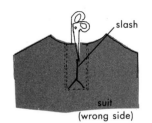

2. The Kangaroo Pocket.

THE SIDE FACINGS. Topstitch twill tape to the right side of the pocket ¼″ inside the raw edge of each side. Turn the tape to the inside and topstitch the remaining edge to the wrong side of the pocket.

ATTACHING THE POCKET. With right sides together, position the top of the pocket upside down on the jacket. Stitch the pocket so that the bottom will be flush with the bottom of the jacket when folded down into position.

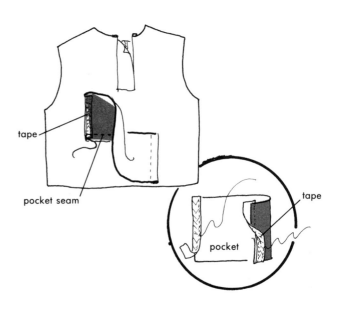

116

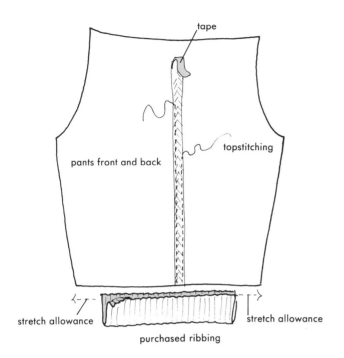

pants front and back

tape

topstitching

stretch allowance

purchased ribbing

stretch allowance

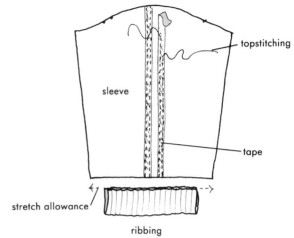

sleeve

topstitching

tape

stretch allowance

ribbing

3. The Action Stripes. Topstitch one or more strips of twill tape to each side of the pants leg and two or more strips to the center of the sleeve, as shown. Finish the bottom of the sleeve and pants leg with purchased ribbing, handling it as you would a self-band.

4. The Full-Fashioned Collar. After joining the shoulder seams, pin and baste the collar to the neck of the jacket, right sides together, ¼″ from the raw edge. Align the front edges of the collar with the placket seams and keep the raw edge of the neck flush with the neck edge of the collar, stretching or compressing the ribbing as necessary for a good fit.

Cut a length of twill tape to equal the neck seam measurement between the placket seams plus ½″ turn-back allowance at either end. Position one long edge of the tape right side up over the collar seam.

Tuck the turnbacks under and topstitch the tape, collar, and jacket together on the seam line.

Turn up the collar and topstitch the remaining edge of the tape to the inside of the jacket.

5. The Waistband. Cut a length of the purchased ribbing to equal the waist measurement, less a 3″ stretch allowance, and seam the short ends. Turn the jacket inside out, slip the seamed ribbing inside, and, with right sides together and raw edges aligned, stretch stitch the waistband seam to finish the bottom of the jacket as for the Boy's Jogging Suit on page 107.

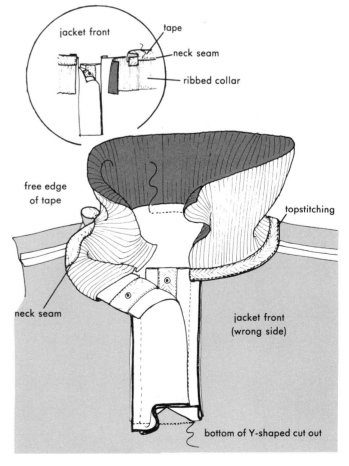

jacket front

tape

neck seam

ribbed collar

free edge of tape

topstitching

neck seam

jacket front (wrong side)

bottom of Y-shaped cut out

117

Infant's "Hippo Bubble" Romper

Early childhood is one of the few times in life that being compared to a hippopotamus is a compliment.

Without the shirt, this little bubble doubles as a sunsuit on the hottest days or, for the coldest days, the pattern can be extended and smocked for an ankle-length jumpsuit made of a cozy double-knit. Similarly extend the raglan sleeve or pair it with the turtleneck.

Smocking a jersey-knit is so easy that you may never return to wovens. The simple geometric hearts and diamonds smocking pattern is ideal for beginners. (If you are a first-time smocker, consult the smocking lesson on page 129.) But, as with all smocking, once the fabric is pleated, any pattern can be embroidered. If you want more of a challenge, you may always substitute one of the other smocking patterns in this book or a tried-and-true favorite of your own.

Materials

Single-knit cotton or cotton-blend jersey fabric: equal to one length of the romper pattern

One skein of six-strand embroidery thread

¼"-wide elastic, four times the child's upper leg measurement

¼ yard snap tape

The Grids

(If unfamiliar with the grid technique see page 180, or substitute any commercial romper or sunsuit pattern with cross-chest gathers and shoulder ties.)

Fold the appropriate grid and trace the romper pattern point-for-point and square-for-square.

The romper has been developed from the pants pattern by adding fullness to the sides and extending the center front to collarbone level.

Fit is controlled by the shoulder ties and leg elastic, so don't worry unnecessarily about measurements or alterations. If you want to alter the pattern, however, measure the baby from the collarbone to the top of the shoulder blade, *including diapers,* and add or subtract whatever you desire within the shaded area.

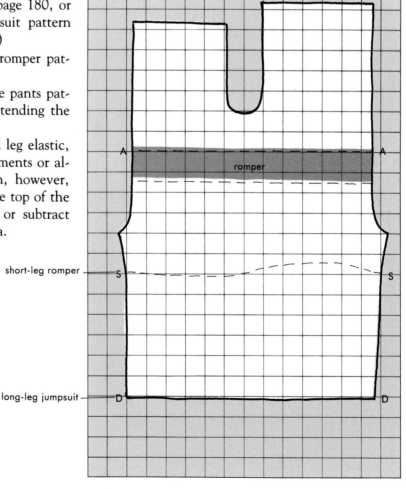

short-leg romper

long-leg jumpsuit

Layout and Cutting

Fold the fabric in half lengthwise and cut the romper as shown. If your jersey comes in tube form, don't fold it in any way. Simply lay it on the table, place the romper patterns on top of the existing folds and cut.

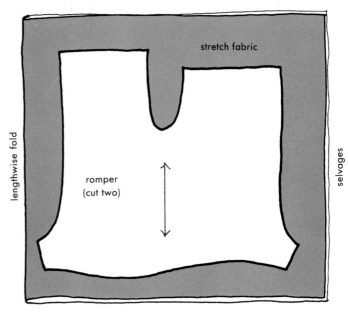

Sewing the Romper

1. Preparing to Smock.

THE SEAMS. Join the two halves of the romper at center front and center back.

HEMMING THE TOP EDGE. Use your zigzag machine to stitch a shell hem at the top of front and back as follows: Set the zigzag at maximum width and nearly maximum stitch length, say seven or eight stitches per inch.

Stitch the hem wrong side up, folding over a ¼″ hem allowance as you stitch. The needle should catch the left edge of the hem allowance as it zigs and go completely off the fabric as it zags to the right. (Or does it zag to the left and zig to the right? Does the spearmint lose its flavor on the bedpost overnight?) If you don't have a zigzag machine, stitch a narrow topstitched hem instead.

THE PLEATING. Use any preferred method to pleat the front and back of the romper with three gathering rows, starting 1¼″ from the finished edge at the top. Draw the gathers up so that the pleated section is 1″ less than one third of the original measurement. (See page 129).

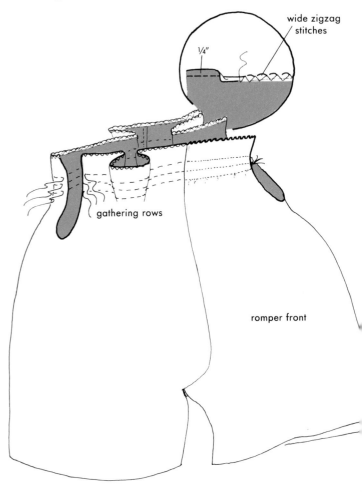

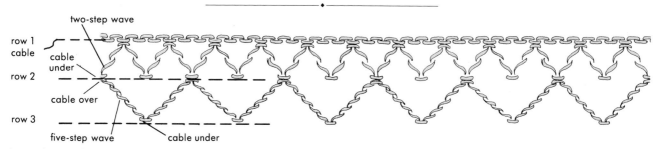

2. Smocking the Pattern.

ROW 1: Cable across the entire row.

ROW 2: Starting the heart pattern: Wave up and down between Rows 1 and 2 with two-step waves, placing the cables at the tops of the waves back-to-back with the cables in the row above.

ROW 3: Completing the hearts: Start with an up cable back-to-back with the down cable at the bottom of the wave in Row 2. Wave down five, cable under. Wave up five times to meet Row 2 again, cable over. Continue across the row to complete the heart pattern.

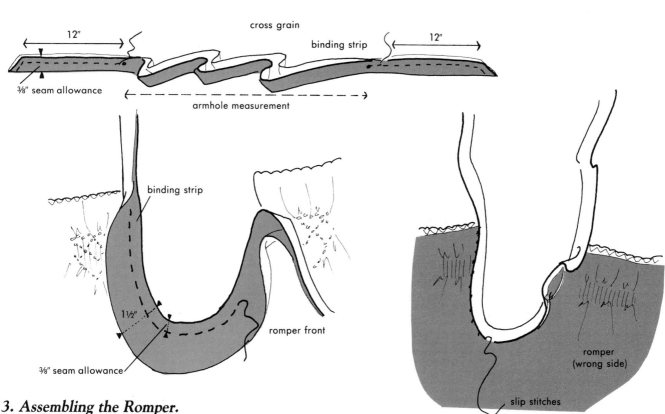

3. Assembling the Romper.

BINDING THE ARMHOLE. Cut two tie extensions on the cross-grain 1½" wide and 24" longer than the armhole measurement. Fold the ties in half lengthwise, right sides together, and seam each of the short ends ⅜" from the raw edges. Leaving the needle in the fabric, raise the presser foot, pivot 90 degrees, and continue stitching for another 12".

Clip the seam allowance and turn the ends of the ties right side out. With right sides together and raw edges aligned, match and stitch the open portion at the cen-

ter of the tie to the armhole, maintaining the ⅜" seam allowance. Turn the free edge of the binding to the inside and hand hem it to the stitches of the armhole seam.

GATHERING THE LEG OPENING. Hem the leg edge of the romper with a shell or topstitched hem as you did the top. Cut a length of ¼" elastic to fit the baby's leg and zigzag it to the inside of the romper 1" above the finished edge.

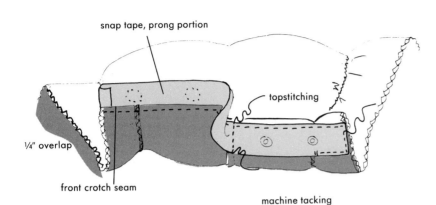

snap tape, prong portion

topstitching

¼" overlap

front crotch seam

machine tacking

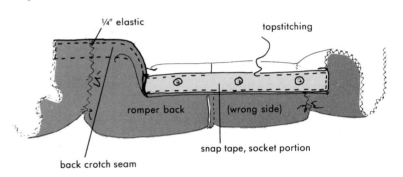

¼" elastic

topstitching

romper back

(wrong side)

back crotch seam

snap tape, socket portion

finished romper

THE CROTCH SEAM. Cut a length of the snap tape to fit the crotch seam, allowing ½" more or less to turn under at each end, depending on the even spacing of the snaps. Turn in the ends and topstitch all four sides of the socket portion face up over the right side of the back crotch seam allowance.

Lay the snap portion of the tape face up over the front so it overlaps the seam allowance by ¼". Turn in the ends and topstitch the overlapped edge. Fold the tape to the inside and secure the remaining three sides to the ruffle below the elastic. Machine tack the center to the center front seam.

Raglan Shirt

The Grid

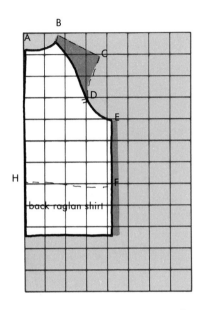

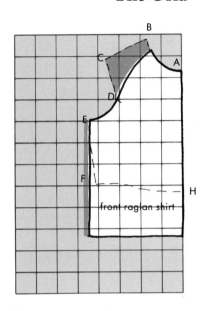

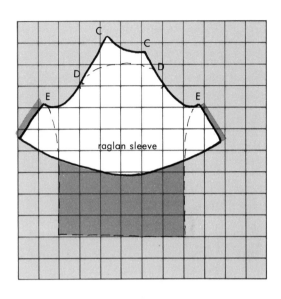

If unfamiliar with the grid technique see page 180 for instructions, or substitute any commercial raglan sleeve pattern designed for stretch fabrics.

Trace the raglan grid point-for-point and square-for-square, transferring any changes you have made to the A–H line of the original sloper. If you made changes to the side seam or armhole depth of the original sloper, enlarge the armhole by extending the C–D–E line of the shirt and sleeve at front and back, as indicated by the shaded area.

Layout and Cutting

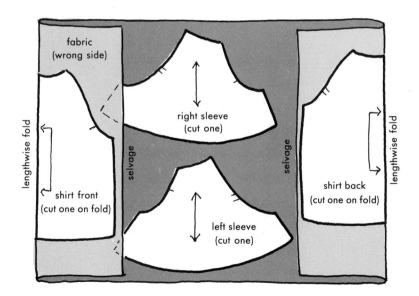

Gate fold the fabric so that the selvages are parallel but do not meet in the center. Cut each sleeve from a single thickness and cut the shirt front and back pieces on the lengthwise folds according to the general principles of the illustrated layout.

Sewing the Shirt

1. The Raglan Seams

The raglan sleeve is named for Lord Raglan who injured his arm in battle and asked his tailor to invent a looser armhole with no shoulder seam to accommodate his bandages.

HEMMING THE SLEEVES. Hem the bottoms of the sleeves as you did the romper top and legs.

CLOSING THE SEAMS. Pin the front edge of each sleeve to either side of the shirt front and join the seams. Trim the seam allowances to ¼", finishing them or not as your preference dictates.

Similarly seam the back of the left sleeve to the shirt back. Join the right back raglan seam from the under-arm to the notch. Trim the seam allowance below the notch but leave the full ¾" seam allowance above it to support the snap closing.

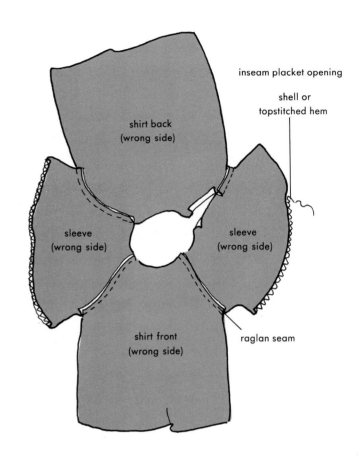

shirt back
(wrong side)

inseam placket opening

shell or
topstitched hem

sleeve
(wrong side)

sleeve
(wrong side)

shirt front
(wrong side)

raglan seam

2. The Neck.

BINDING THE CREW NECK. Cut the binding strip on the cross-grain, 1½" wide, and 1½" less than the neck seam measurement. Fold it in half lengthwise, wrong sides together. Stretch seam it to the outside of the neck, matching all raw edges at the raglan seam and the neck and distributing the fullness evenly throughout.

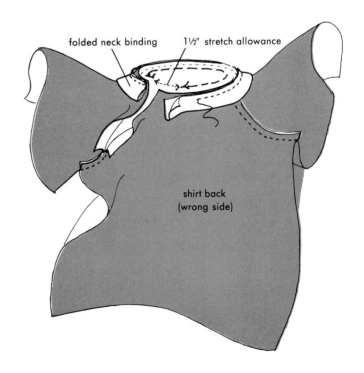

folded neck binding

1½" stretch allowance

shirt back
(wrong side)

3. The Inseam Placket. Cut a length of the snap tape to fit the open portion of the remaining raglan seam plus 1″. Separate the tape, and turn the raw edge under at the top. Matching the turnunder to the neck edge of the binding on the right side of the sleeve, lay the socket portion face up over the seam allowance, right edge flush with the seam line. Tuck the free end inside the seam below the notch. Edgestitch the two long edges and the top of the tape to the seam allowance.

Similarly place the prong portion of the tape to the seam allowance on the shirt back, and edgestitch the left edge to the seam line. Turn the tape to the inside and edgestitch the remaining long edge and the top to the shirt. Snap the tape closed and bar tack all layers together where the placket opens above the seam.

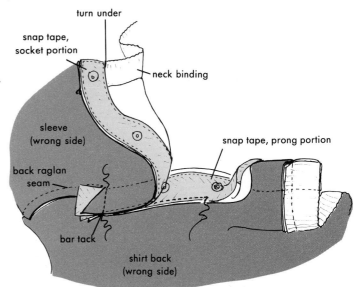

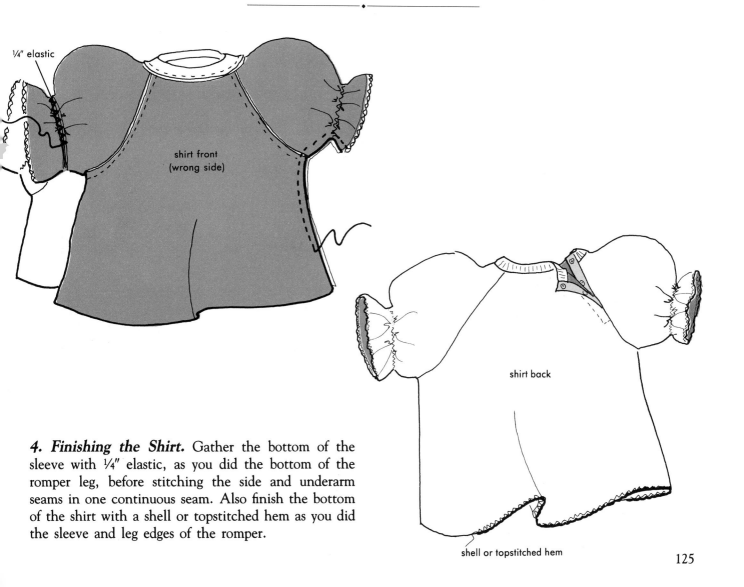

4. Finishing the Shirt. Gather the bottom of the sleeve with ¼″ elastic, as you did the bottom of the romper leg, before stitching the side and underarm seams in one continuous seam. Also finish the bottom of the shirt with a shell or topstitched hem as you did the sleeve and leg edges of the romper.

125

Summer and Sunshine

mocking is beautiful, practical, durable, and fun to do. Like other needle arts, the basics are easy, the possibilities are endless, and the origins are threaded through history.

Modern smocking is descended from the traditional farmers' smocks of nineteenth-century rural England. Students of costume history might speculate that these farmers' smocks are descended from burlap feedbags worn pillow-case style, a hole cut in the top for the head and the arms sticking out side slits. The trouble with this cut, well known to any pillow-case ghost at Halloween, is a tendency for the excess width to fall off the shoulders.

The remedy, perhaps slow to come, was quick and practical: bind the excess fabric into folds across the chest and back with twine, perhaps repeating the process at wrist and forearm to keep the hoe from catching in the sleeve. The "smock" was born. Gradually, coarsely bound folds became embroidered pleats and the embroidery on the pleats evolved into more elaborate patterns, some even incorporating wagon wheels or staffs of wheat to signify the wearer's trade.

So, too, fabrics became more varied and of finer stuff until Sunday smocks became common. A well-known author of the period, Thomas Hardy, in *Under the Greenwood Tree*, tells of the practice of local churches keeping a supply on hand to replace the everyday slop smock for the gentlemen of the choir.

Today we smock mostly finer fabrics for children's wear, and although the stitches of yesterday are still popular in tradi-

Mary Cassatt's 1884 painting of children at the beach shows them totally absorbed in the center of their own world, oblivious to the commerce and vastness of the world about them, the sky a blue stripe at the top as in a child's drawing, stretching as endlessly as a child's concept of time.

tional geometric designs, the exciting colors of modern dyes and the availability of superior embroidery floss have inspired the relatively new art of picture smocking.

IF YOU HAVE NOT SMOCKED BEFORE

Pretend for a moment that you are the practical genius of yore, determined to pleat the burlap feedbag into a successful smock. You would thread a needle, bring it up through the cloth where you wanted to start the gathering, pinch up a pleat, put the needle through it, pinch up another pleat, and bind that to the first in much the same way you might bind a row of sticks together for a fence. When you had gathered up the excess fullness, you would put the needle through to the back again and knot the twine securely. This is still the basic idea of smocking today, although we get neater and more regular pleats by pleating the fabric before embroidering the design.

Let's also pretend that you naturally looped the thread off to your right to keep it out of the way as you poked your needle through each pleat, and that when you were through all the stitches made a nice, even, regular pattern. You might even have been curious to see how it would look to change the thread position and then looped it under the needle for a few stitches. A neighboring wife, following your lead, might have tried alternating the thread position with every stitch, looping the thread over the needle for one stitch and under the needle for the next, imitating the look of cables in a chain. Pleased with the success of your idea and not wanting to be outdone, you might then have experimented and moved your needle up or down to a new level before taking up the next pleat, and liked that look, too.

Many such inventions have contributed to the art of smocking as we know it today. But who would have suspected that the infinite variety and creative possibilities of three simple ideas (binding pleats together, varying the position of the thread in relation to the needle, and varying the level of the needle in relation to the previous stitch) would have endured into the twentieth century and, by last count in 1984, inspired more than 10,000 people to become members of The Smocking Arts Guild of America.

TECHNIQUES
Smocking Techniques

Modern smocking pre-pleats the fabric with regular rows of gathering stitches before working the embroidery. Allow three times the desired finished width for traditional smocking, slightly more for picture smocking or very fine fabrics.

Modern Pleaters. By far the best way to pre-pleat the fabric is to run it between the rollers of a small pleating machine. These machines are readily available at smocking-supply stores and are well worth the reasonable cost if you are planning to do much smocking. If you are just testing the waters, so to speak, the same shops invariably offer pleating services, many by mail, at modest cost. Consult the mail-order sources in the Appendix for further information.

Transfer Dots. Before widespread use of the pleater, transfer dots were available, and many shops still offer these. Consult the mail-order sources for a smocking-supply store in your area or purchase a pattern with transfer dots included from one of the major pattern companies.

Cut as many rows of dots as the number of gathering rows you want and iron them onto the wrong side of the fabric.

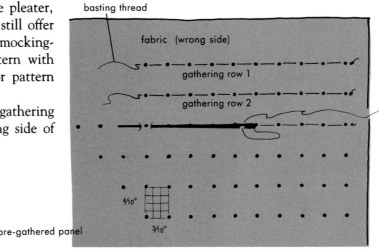

Connect the dots in each row with strong basting thread, passing the needle just under the circle of the dot. When all rows are basted, pull up the threads to the measurement given in your pattern.

Quadrille-paper Dots. If you have no access to other pleating methods, you can draw your own transfer dots with a hot-transfer embroidery pencil onto quadrille paper marked with ten squares to the inch. Allow three spaces between the horizontal dots and four spaces between vertical rows. Transfer the dots to the wrong side of the fabric with a hot iron and gather.

A Practice Sampler. Cut an 8″ strip from the width of a piece of broadcloth, pleat it by any preferred method, and draw it up to 1″ less than one third the original width. Knot the ends of the gathering threads securely at both sides.

Learning the Stitches

Each row of smocking is worked from the right side, moving pleat by pleat from left to right across the row, picking up one more pleat with each stitch.

The needle is always held parallel to the gathering rows, pointing left (unless you are left handed, in which case the directions are reversed). Take the stitch through the upper third of each pleat, entering from the right and emerging in the valley on the left.

Try for a nice, balanced look to the stitches as you pull up the thread after each one. Too much tension will distort the pleats and show too much fabric; too little will look droopy.

Starting. Smocking is worked on the right side of the fabric. Cut a length of six-strand embroidery thread no longer than your arm. Separate the strands from each other and thread the needle with three. Knot the end of the thread and bring the needle up into one of the valleys at the left edge of the right side of the fabric.

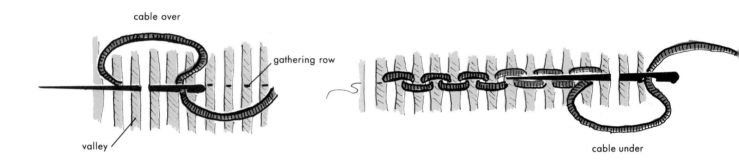

The Cable Stitch.

CABLE OVER. Bring the needle up in one of the valleys at the level of the first gathering row. Loop the thread over the needle, straddle the valley, and pick up the next pleat to the right, as shown.

CABLE UNDER. Loop the thread under the needle before picking up the next pleat.

Complete the row, alternating cable over and cable under.

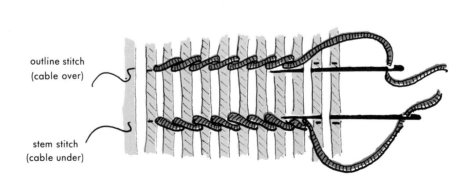

Variations.

OUTLINE STITCH. Cable over the entire row.

STEM STITCH. Cable under the entire row.

BACK SMOCK. Cable on the wrong side of the panel (stitches are invisible from the right side, but stabilize pleats in unsmocked areas of picture smocking).

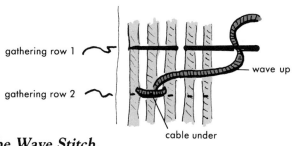

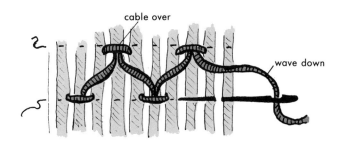

The Wave Stitch.

WAVE UP. Starting at the level of Gathering Row 3, bring the needle up at the left edge of the panel, as before. Cable under. Raise the needle up to the level of Gathering Row 2 and, keeping the needle parallel to the gathering row, pick up the next pleat, entering from the right, picking up the top third of the pleat, and emerging in the valley as before. Cable over at the new level.

WAVE DOWN. Return the needle to the starting level and pick up the next pleat. Cable under. Continue across the row, waving up and down between the *under* cables at the level of Row 3 and the *over* cables at the level of Row 2.

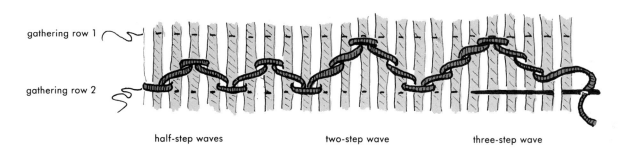

half-step waves   two-step wave   three-step wave

Variations.

HALF-STEP WAVES. Wave only half a space up or down.

TWO- OR THREE-STEP WAVES. Wave up or down in two or three steps before cabling at the new level.

Ending. Always end in the valley *under* a cable stitch.

Put the needle to the back in the valley under the last stitch. Take two back stitches on the wrong side of the same pleat to secure the thread.

Blocking. Remove the gathering threads, pin the panel to the ironing board and, holding the iron about an inch above the panel, steam the pleats into uniform alignment.

Using the Stitches

Traditional Smocking. Infinite combinations of cable and wave stitches form the interlocking geometric shapes of traditional smocking. Find diamond points in the collar of the Velvet Party Dress, hearts in the "Hippo Bubble" Romper, and rectangles in the Smocked Bonnet.

Picture Smocking. Picture smocking is one of the cre-

ative new developments of modern smocking. Here, the pleats are your canvas, the needle your brush, the richly varied colors of modern floss your artist's palette.

There are two kinds of picture smocking. In the farmer's-garden design of the smocked sunsuit, rows of cable stitches stacked back-to-back on top of each other form solid blocks of color. The Dutch-milkmaid design of the pinafore is drawn with stacked waves.

Smocked Bonnet

This bonnet is so easy to smock and sew that it makes a good beginner's project or last minute gift. The marvelously flexible smocking will adapt to almost any size head and the depth of the back panel can be adjusted by increasing or decreasing the seam allowance.

As with all smocking, once the panel is pleated it can be smocked in any pattern, so if you prefer more smocking, you may adapt one of the other patterns in the book to the bonnet.

If another pattern calls for fewer gathering rows, make up the difference with an extra row of cables at the top or bottom of the design, being sure to have a cable row along Gathering Rows 1 and 9 so that the front and back of the panel will ruffle attractively.

You could also substitute the vegetables from the farmer's garden for the flowers in the window boxes.

Materials

½ yard percale, broadcloth, or lawn

Six-strand embroidery floss: One skein of light blue; scraps of green, red, orange, scarlet, yellow

Two small pearlized shank buttons

Layout and Cutting

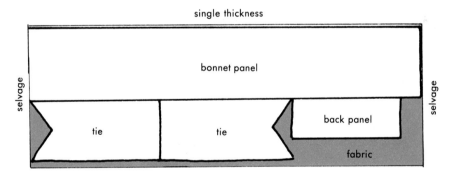

single thickness

bonnet panel

selvage

tie   tie   back panel

fabric

selvage

(The layout is so simple that no grid is necessary.)

Cut from the width of the fabric one 7½" strip for the smocked panel, two 18" × 6½" strips for the ties, and one 4" × 12" piece for the back panel.

Preparing to Smock. Stitch ¼" hems along both long edges of the panel. Pleat it with nine rows of gathering threads, spaced ⅜" apart starting 1¼" from the front edge, and pull up the gathers to a measurement of 13".

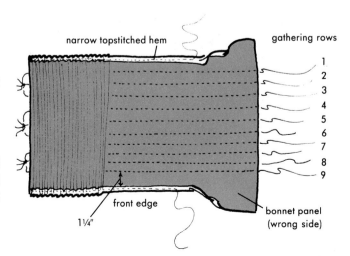

narrow topstitched hem

gathering rows

1
2
3
4
5
6
7
8
9

front edge

1¼"

bonnet panel
(wrong side)

133

Smocking the Design

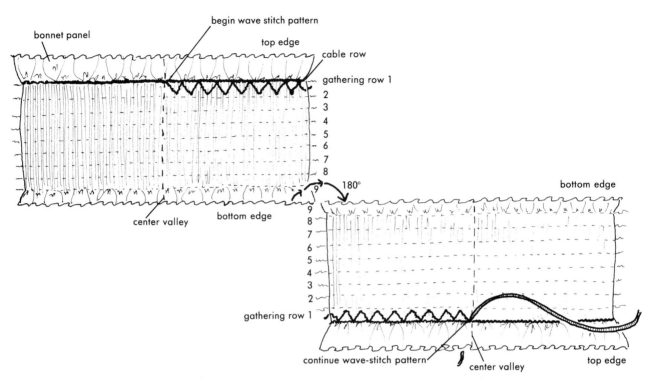

This design is a wonderful example of the fascination of traditional geometric designs. Smock everything except the flowers in the window boxes with light blue.

Top Border. Cable across Gathering Row 1.

The Diamonds.

ROW 1. The design must be centered in order to balance the number of window boxes on both sides. Count the number of *under* cables in the top row and mark the valley beneath the one nearest the center with a row of basting stitches. Slide the needle down to the level of Gathering Row 2, bring it up in the valley to the left of the basted center valley, cable under. Wave up three, and cable over [back-to-back] with the under cable in the previous row. Wave back down to the level of Row 2, cable under. Repeat the wave pattern to the end of the row, tucking the upper points back-to-back with the cable row at the level of Row 1, as shown.

FINISHING THE ROW. Turn the work 180 degrees so it is upside down. Bring the needle up in the basted valley under the first stitch and wave down three to the cable row. Cable under, wave up three, cable over, and continue the pattern to the other end of the row. When the wave row is complete, it will look as if it had been worked in one continuous row.

ROW 2. Return the panel to normal position and resume the wave pattern beneath the last stitch at the left of the previous row, waving up and down as before, but in contrary motion so that a pattern of diamonds gradually emerges.

The Window Boxes. Two rows worked in contrary motion form a series of four one-step diamonds linking the boxes together. Three-step waves form the sides of the boxes, groups of cables outline the tops and bottoms, and the center peaks are small two-step waves.

TOP ROW. Start at the center pleat. Cable over. Wave up one and cable over midway between Gathering Rows 5 and 4. Wave down, cable under. Repeat, to form a second link.

Start the box. Wave up three, cable over, cable nine, wave up two, and cable over the peak midway between Gathering Rows 4 and 3. Wave back down, cable under, cable nine, wave down three, cable under,

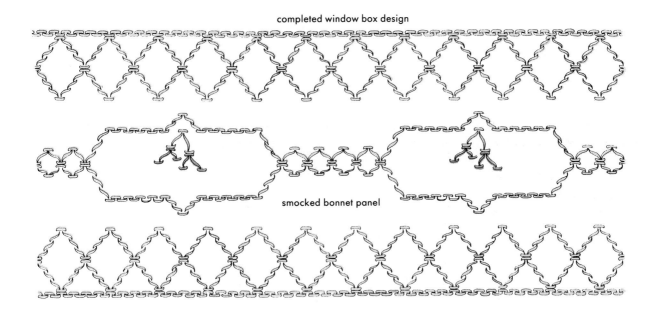

completed window box design

smocked bonnet panel

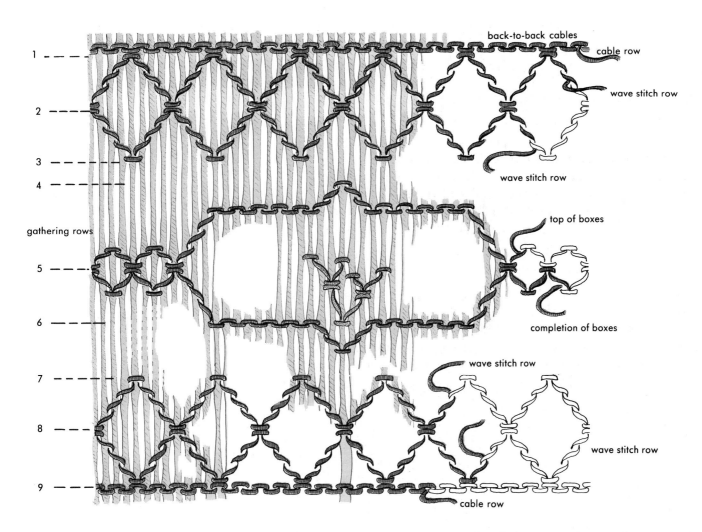

and finish the pattern with two more one-step wave links. Continue alternating links and boxes across the row. Turn the work 180 degrees and finish the row as you did the top row of the diamonds.

BOTTOM ROW. Similarly return the panel to normal position. Start at the left edge and resume the link-and-box pattern in contrary motion across the row. Now you see the fascination of the geometric designs!

Bottom Border. Once again, turn the work and repeat the directions for the top border.

The Blossoms. Borrow the blossoms and leaves from the flowers surrounding the Dutch milkmaid on the Smocked Pinafore on page 139.

Sewing the Bonnet

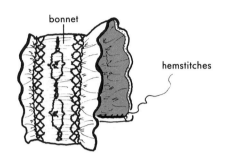

The Panel. Remove the gathering threads and steam block the panel to set the pleats. Turn up a small edge at either end of the panel and hem the selvage to the inside.

The Ties. Fold the ties in half lengthwise, wrong sides together, and stitch the long sides together ¼" inside the raw edges, following the diagonal shaping across one end. Trim, turn, and press.

Fold in the raw edges of the remaining short ends, fold a pleat or two, and secure them to the inside of the bonnet at a 45 degree angle to the top row of smocking.

The Back Panel. Fold the panel in half crosswise, and stitch the two sides together ¼" from the raw edges. Trim, turn, and press. Fold in the raw edges of the remaining short side, center it in the back edge of the smocked panel, and hem it to the last row of smocking.

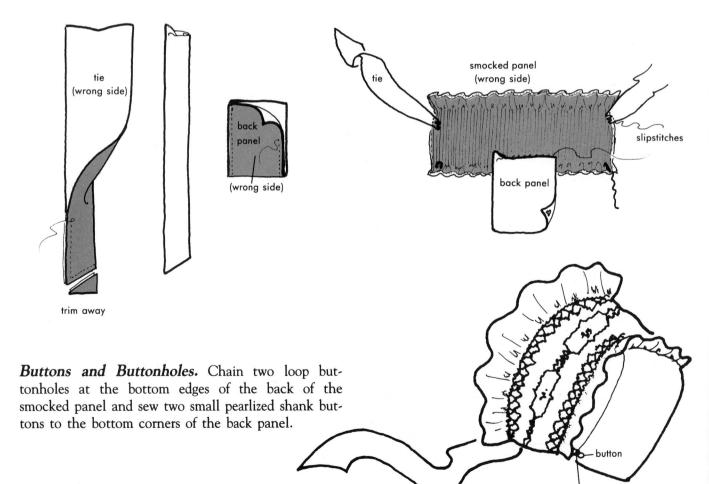

Buttons and Buttonholes. Chain two loop buttonholes at the bottom edges of the back of the smocked panel and sew two small pearlized shank buttons to the bottom corners of the back panel.

Smocked Pinafore

Smocked Pinafore

The pinafore leaves the shoulder open and carries the pillow-case idea one step further toward ease and practicality.

Cut two identical rectangles, smock the pleats across the chest in any pattern you choose, sew up the sides, hem the top and bottom, add shoulder ties, and you have a sundress, pinafore, apron, or summer nightgown.

Be sure to include a deep hem allowance because the elasticity of the smocking will expand to slip on over the head and will recover to fit snugly around the chest for as long as the fabric lasts.

On this pinafore, the Dutch milkmaid stands amidst the traditional flowers of Holland, tulips and daffodils. Crisp shoulder ties echo the shape of the windmill behind her.

Materials

White broadcloth, percale, or lawn: double the desired pinafore length plus ½ yard hem and tie allowance

Six-strand embroidery floss: One skein each of light blue, yellow, medium blue, green; scraps of red, orange, scarlet, brown

Layout and Cutting

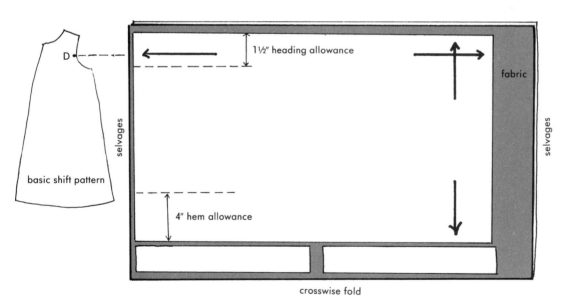

(No grid is necessary. There are only two skirt rectangles and four shoulder ties to this pattern.)

The Length of the Rectangle. Measure the shift from point D at the armhole curve to the hemline, or measure the child from arm joint to mid-thigh. Add a 1½″ heading allowance and a nice, deep, bottom hem allowance of 4″ or so.

The Width. Measure the distance from point D to the

A–H line and mark point X. Multiply the D–X measurement by six. Use this measurement for the width of the rectangle if it is significantly smaller than the width of the fabric; otherwise, simply cut the length of the rectangle from selvage to selvage.

The Ties. The width of the cut ties is 3″. Add 12″ to the D–C measurement for the length.

Smocking the Design

Preparation. Narrowly hem the tops of both rectangles before pleating with seven rows of gathering thread, spacing the first row 1¼″ from the hemmed edge. Pull up the gathers to equal the D–D measurement.

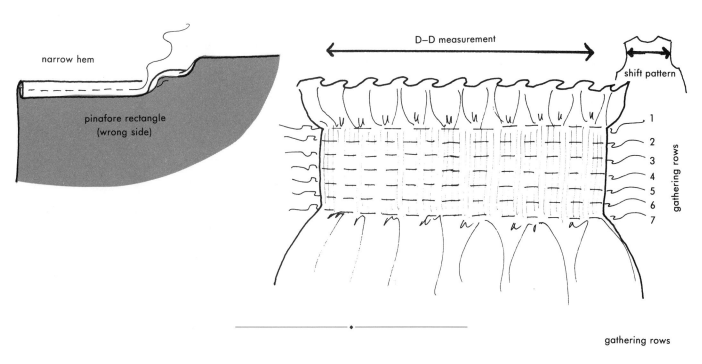

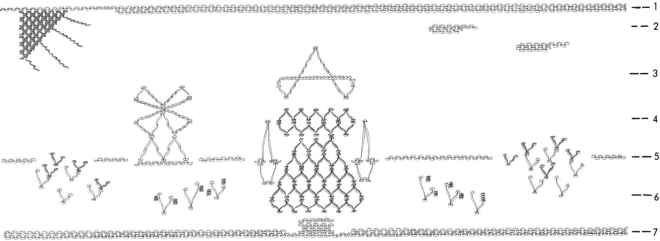

completed milkmaid design

Grass and Sky. Smock the sun, clouds, sky, and grass on front and back panels exactly as described for the Boy's Smocked Sunsuit on page 144.

Back Smocking. Turn work to wrong side. With white, cable the portions of Gathering Rows 2, 3, 4 and 6 that have not been incorporated into picture on front to stabilize pleats after gathering threads are removed.

CANAL. Cable across Gathering Row 5 with light blue, omitting cables behind flowers, windmill, and maid, to add depth perspective.

The Milkmaid. Center the figure over the center valley and build the design from the bottom up.

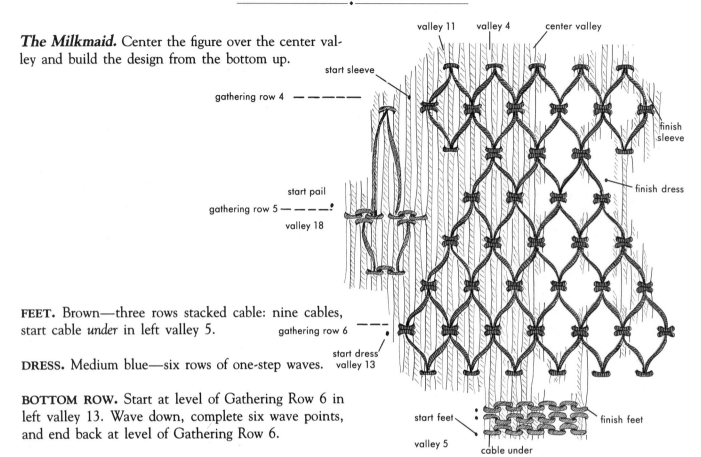

FEET. Brown—three rows stacked cable: nine cables, start cable *under* in left valley 5.

DRESS. Medium blue—six rows of one-step waves.

BOTTOM ROW. Start at level of Gathering Row 6 in left valley 13. Wave down, complete six wave points, and end back at level of Gathering Row 6.

CONTINUE. Start next row back-to-back with first stitch of bottom row. Wave up, again complete six points. Similarly start next three rows back-to-back with points of previous rows, making one less point in each row and spacing the rows, as shown, until the three points of the last row are located approximately one third of the way between Gathering Rows 4 and 5.

SLEEVES. Bring the needle up in left valley 11 at the level of Gathering Row 4. Cable over, wave down five points. The bottoms of the center three points will touch the three points of the last row of the dress.

TOP ROW. Wave up five points to complete the sleeve diamonds.

Hat. Two rows, yellow.

FRONT VIEW ON FRONT PANEL. Bring needle up at level of Gathering Row 3 in same valley as start of sleeve. Cable over, wave down one step, cable under. Wave up seven to level of Gathering Row 2. Cable over, wave down seven. Cable under, wave one step back up to level of Gathering Row 3, cable over.

BRIM. Cable under back-to-back with first stitch of previous row, cable over 17, end row with cable under back-to-back with last stitch of previous row.

BACK VIEW. Cable under entire brim on back panel.

PIGTAILS. Yellow bullion stitches, as shown.

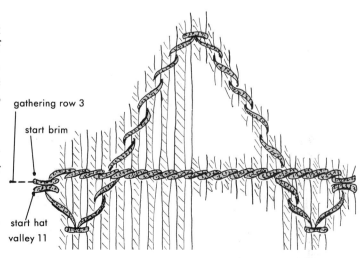

Windmill. Six rows, medium brown.

The windmill covers 14 valleys and should be centered between the milkmaid and the sun. The bottom of the lower windmill blade and the top of the mill are combined in one row.

BASE. Cable 15 at level of Gathering Row 5, starting and ending cable under.

MILL. First row: cable under, wave up two, cable over midway between Gathering Rows 5 and 4, wave down two, cable under. Repeat.

BEGIN BLADE. Slide needle up center of first windmill pleat, cable over midway between Gathering Rows 5 and 4. Angle down to point of first windmill wave with cabling over continuously, as you did for the sunrays. Cable under, wave up two, cable over at level of Gathering Row 4 to complete the windmill, wave down two, wave back up to starting level with cable under.

COMPLETE BLADE. Cable under back-to-back with first blade stitch, wave up to peak of windmill, wave back down, cable under.

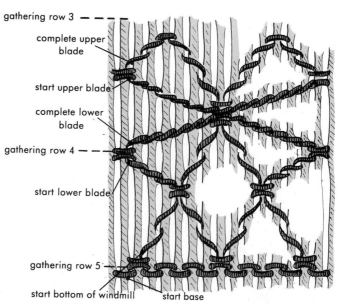

TOP BLADE. Slide needle up starting valley to slightly below level of Gathering Row 3. Cable over, wave down to peak of windmill, cable under, wave back up.

FINAL ROW. Cable under, wave up two, cable over, wave down to peak of windmill, cable over, complete row in reverse order.

FLOWERS. (all leaves are green): Cable over, wave down as far as desired, cable under same pleat, wave up as far as desired, cable over.

Repeat pattern and scatter blossoms in varied colors for tulips. Cable over same pleat three or four times in yellow to tuck daffodil blossoms beneath leaves.

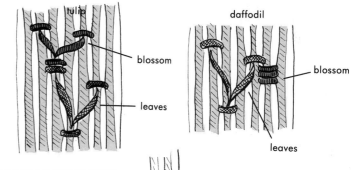

Milk Pails. Two rows, medium brown.

HANDLES. Slide the needle down valley 18 and bring it up at level of Gathering Row 5. Cable under, over, under, wave up to Gathering Row 4, cable over on the same pleat, wave back down, cable under on the same pleat, cable over, cable under.

PAILS. Bring the needle up in the valley beneath the first handle stitch (valley 17). Cable over, wave down the same pleat, cable under, over, under, wave up on the same pleat, cable over beneath the middle handle stitch.

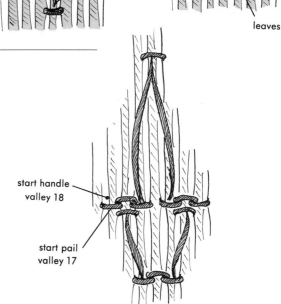

Sewing the Pinafore

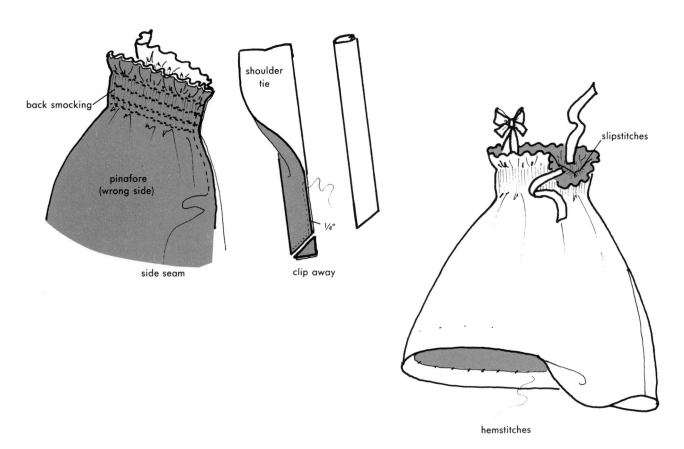

The Side Seams. Remove the gathering threads and steam and block the smocking. Match both sides of the rectangles to each other, wrong sides together, and stitch the side seams, finishing them in any way you prefer.

The Ties. Fold the ties in half lengthwise, wrong sides together, and stitch them ¼″ from the raw edges and diagonally across the bottoms, as the dotted line indi-cates. Trim the seam, turn, and press. Slipstitch the ties to the top row of smocking midway between the center of the smocked panel and the side seam.

The Hem. Turn up whatever hem allowance you planned and stitch it by machine or hand. Hand hem stitches don't show as much when the hem is let down next year.

Boy's Smocked Sunsuit

Boy's Smocked Sunsuit

The diligent farmer in the smocked inset has raised a healthy crop of vegetables, proving that "The best fertilizer is the gardener's own shadow."

Carrots and radishes flourish under the soil, corn and tomatoes above it. Tomato-shaped buttons at the side closing complete the picture.

If you feel that white is an impractical color for a little boy's sunsuit or if you prefer a more everyday look, you can choose a bright fabric to color coordinate with one of the vegetables for the sunsuit and cut the inset from white to smock the picture.

— Materials —

1 yard 42"–45" broadcloth fabric

½ yard of 1"-wide elastic

Two novelty buttons

Six-strand embroidery floss: One skein each of medium blue, medium brown, bright yellow, bright green, light blue; scraps of red, dark red, orange

— The Grids —

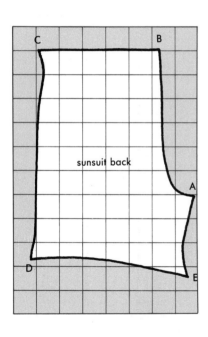
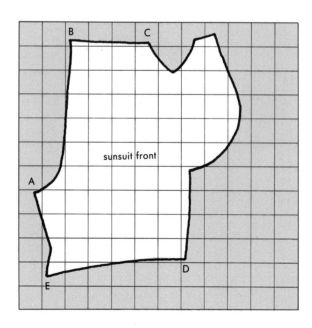
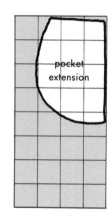

(If unfamiliar with the grid technique see page 180, or substitute any commercial sunsuit pattern with a one-piece bib front.)

THE BASIC PATTERN. Fold the appropriate number of squares in the grid and trace the sunsuit patterns point-for-point and square-for-square. The yoke extension and smocked panel are developed from the front pants sloper; the shaded area in the back represents the casing allowance.

Transfer any changes you have made to the center front and center back, sides, and crotch depth. Cut longer shoulder straps to absorb any minor shoulder-to-waist variations.

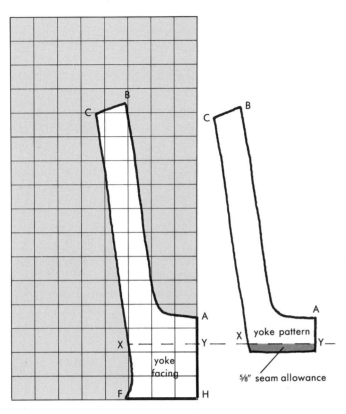

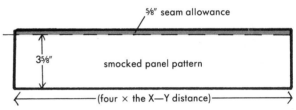

THE SMOCKED PANEL. The smocked panel is always the same depth. Locate the styleline for the yoke seam as follows: Measure 3⅝" up from point H and locate point Y. Square a styleline across the yoke at point Y. Label point X at the intersection of the styleline and the armhole curve. Cut the yoke facing as traced on the grid, adding a ⅝" seam allowance above the styleline. Trace the yoke above the styleline and add ⅝" seam allowance below it for the yoke. Quadruple the X–Y distance and add ⅝" seam allowance above the styleline for the smocked panel pattern.

Layout and Cutting

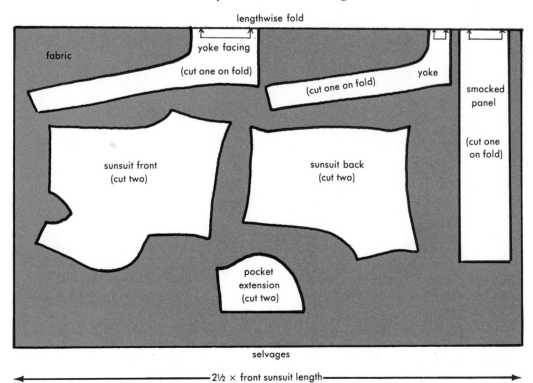

Fold the fabric in half vertically and cut the sunsuit according to the general guidelines of the illustrated layout.

Smocking the Design

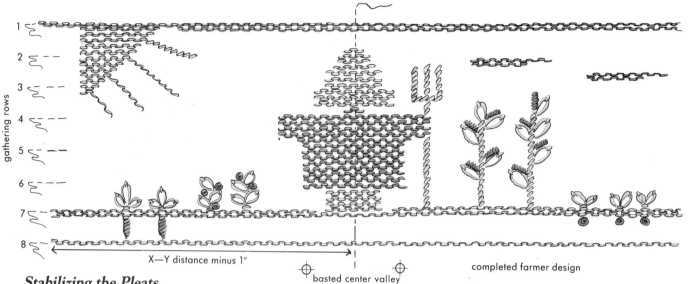

Stabilizing the Pleats.

GATHERING ROW 1. Cable blue (first sky row).

GATHERING ROWS 2–6. Cable white on the wrong side.

GATHERING ROW 7. Cable green (first grass row).

GATHERING ROW 8. Cable brown.

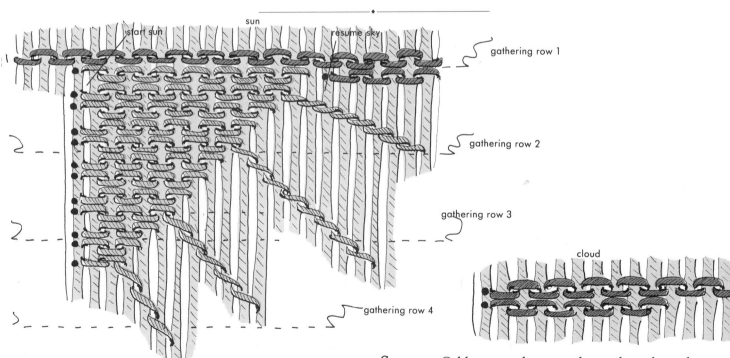

The Sun. Yellow.

TOP ROW. Back-to-back beneath first sky row. Cable 13, start cable over. Work ten more rows, diminishing one stitch each row.

BOTTOM ROW. Cable two, end cable over.

Sunrays. Cable over, changing the angle and number of stitches, as shown.

CLOUDS. Blue.

TOP ROW. Cable 13, start cable under.

BOTTOM ROW. Cable nine.

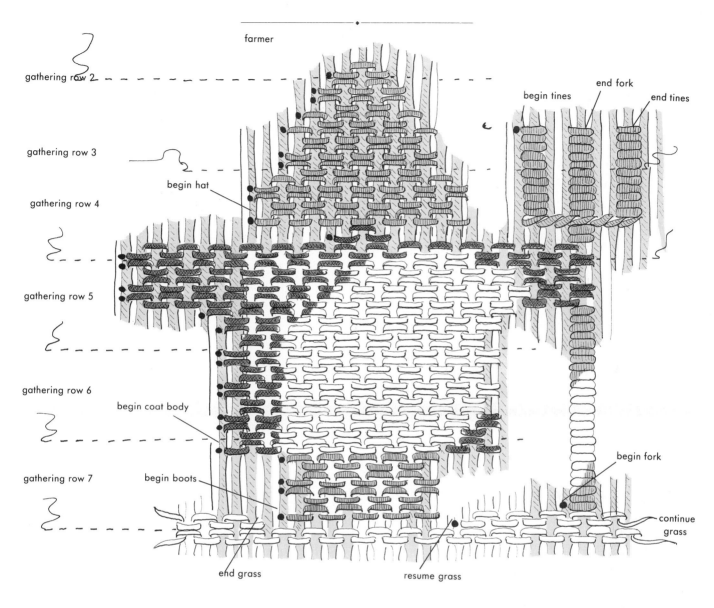

The Farmer. Stack cable rows from the bottom up, starting just above grass on Row 7.

BOOTS. Four rows, brown: Cable nine, start cable under.

COAT. Medium blue.
Body: eight rows (hem of coat at level of Gathering Row 6): Cable 17, start cable under.
Underarm: one row: Cable 19, start over.
Sleeve: four rows (shoulders at level of Gathering Row 4): Cable 29, start over.
Collar: one row: cable three, start under.

HAT. Brown.
Brim: three rows: Cable 13, start under.
Hat: three rows: Cable nine, start over.
Crown: one row: Cable seven, start over.
Two rows: Cable five.

Top row: Cable three (top of crown at level of Gathering Row 2).

The Fork. Cable over two pleats from top to bottom for center. Begin tines at same level and allow two valleys to show between tines. Cable over to join outer tines.

Completing the Grass. Cable above first grass row at Gathering Row 7, stopping two valleys before the farmer and continuing two valleys beyond him, as shown.

Completing the Sky. Cable at Row 1, just below the first sky row, starting with blue two valleys beyond the last yellow sun cable, as shown.

147

The Vegetables.

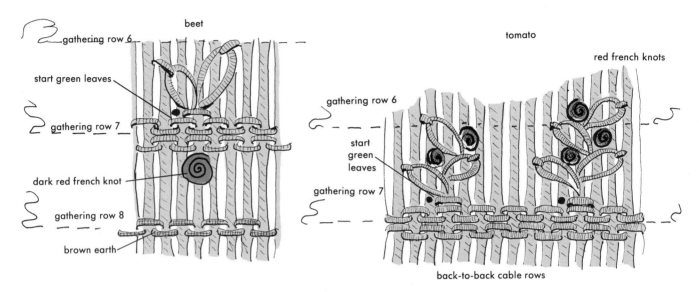

RADISHES. Two green lazy daisy leaves above ground, dark red French knots below.

TOMATOES. Lazy daisy leaf formation above the ground, red French knots in leaves.

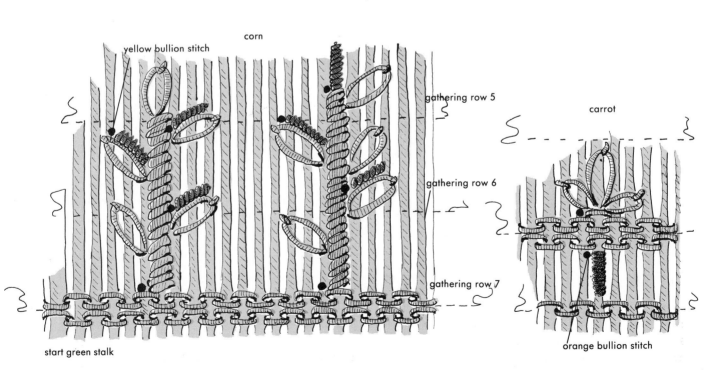

CORN. Ascend valley of same two pleats with cable under for stalks, lazy daisy leaves, yellow bullion stitch ears.

CARROTS. Three lazy daisy leaves above the ground, orange bullion stitches below.

Sewing the Sunsuit

1. The Yoke Seam.

BLOCKING THE PANEL. When the smocking is completed, remove the gathering rows. Place the upper yoke piece and the panel near each other on the ironing board, allowing the pleats to expand as necessary until the panel and the upper yoke seam are the same width. Block the panel and set the pleats with an iron (on full steam) held just above the panel for a minute or two.

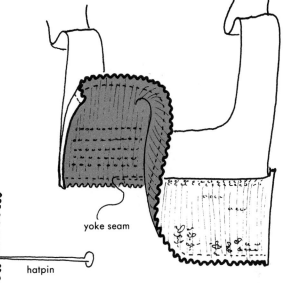
yoke seam

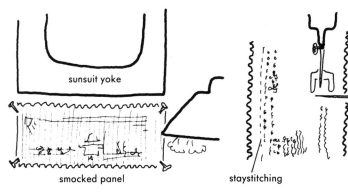
sunsuit yoke

smocked panel

staystitching

hatpin

STAYSTITCHING. Staystitch the panel ⅛″ above and below the top and bottom smocking rows, pushing the pleats under the presser foot of the machine with a hat-

pin or the point of a seam ripper as you stitch to hold the pleats at right angles to the smocking rows and prevent them from stretching out of alignment during seaming. With right sides together, align the raw edge of the top of the smocked panel over the edge of the yoke seam and stitch the panel to the yoke. Press the seam allowance up toward the yoke and set it aside.

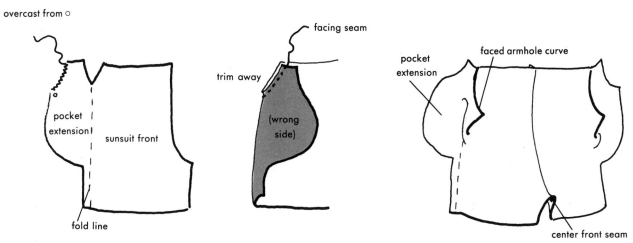
overcast from ○

pocket extension

sunsuit front

fold line

facing seam

trim away

(wrong side)

pocket extension

faced armhole curve

center front seam

2. The Pants Front.

FACING THE ARMHOLE. Neatly finish the top of the left front pocket extension with a narrow hem or a row of machine overcasting above the ○. Fold the extension over the pants front, right sides together, using the side seam line as a fold guide and making sure that all the raw edges of the armhole cutouts are aligned.

Stitch the facing seam from the fold at the side seam

to the raw edge of the yoke seam, clip the corner, turn the facing to the inside and press.

THE CENTER FRONT SEAM. Similarly face the right armhole before joining the center front seam. Overcast the seam close to the seam line before trimming the allowance to ¼″.

3. The Pants Back.

THE ELASTIC CASING. Join the pants back at the center back seam and finish the seam as you did the front. Turn the casing to the inside along the fold line, turn up a ¼″ hem, and topstitch the edge of the casing to the pants.

Cut a piece of ¾″ elastic to a length 1″ less than the back waist measurement. Fasten a safety pin at a right angle to each end of the elastic and thread it through the casing.

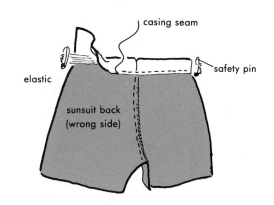

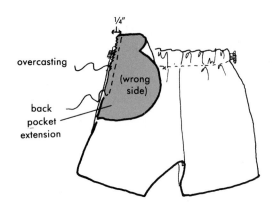

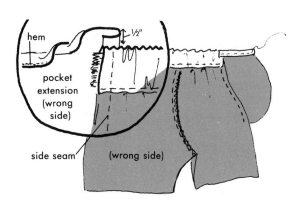

THE BACK POCKET EXTENSION. Pin the back pocket extension to the back pants, right sides together, matching the raw edges at the side seam, but allowing the pocket to extend ½″ beyond the casing at the top.

Stitch the seam ¼″ away from the raw edge, simultaneously closing the open ends of the casing and securing the elastic within.

Overcast the seam and press it outward over the pocket. Finish the top with a machine stitched ¼″ double hem.

4. Finishing the Placket Pocket.

CLOSING THE POCKETS. Match the front and the back, right sides together, along the length of the side seam and the rounded outer edges of the pockets. Stitch the rounded edges of the placket pockets starting at the ○ and ending at the top of the back pocket extension, as shown.

THE SIDE AND CROTCH SEAMS. Close the side seams, starting the stitching 1½″ above the dot and continuing to the bottom of the leg. Overcast and trim these seams, also. Turn the pocket placket to the inside and, with the pants still inside out, close and finish the crotch seam.

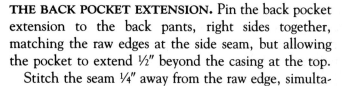

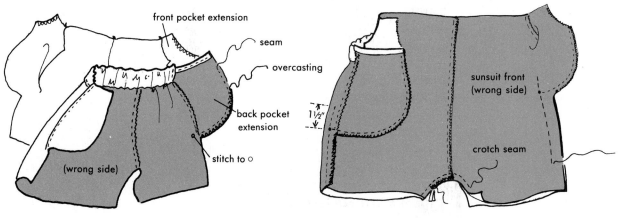

5. The Yoke.

THE YOKE SEAM. Retrieve the upper yoke and smocked panel assembly. Pin the bottom edge of the panel to the front of the pants, with right sides together and raw edges aligned, and stitch the seam as you seamed the panel to the upper yoke, following the staystitches as a seam guide. Press pants seam allowance down over panel.

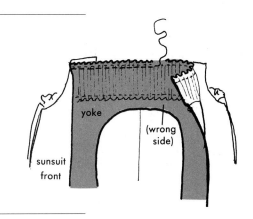

THE FACING. Pin the yoke facing to the right side of the assembled sunsuit and seam all around the outer edges of the straps and neckline ¼" away from the raw edges. Clip the seam at the neckline curve and turn the facing right side out. Hem the free edge of the yoke to the seam allowance on the inside.

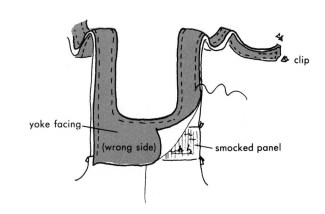

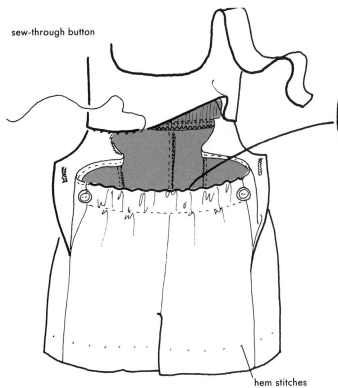

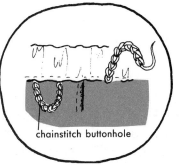

6. Finishing the Sunsuit.

BUTTONS AND BUTTONHOLES. Work chainstitch buttonholes on the inside of the back casing 1" away from the center and make machine buttonholes to close the pocket placket at the side front.

Measure the shoulder strap and sew the buttons to hold them snugly without sliding off the shoulder. Sew the side-closing buttons on top of the casing on the outside of the back.

HEMMING THE LEG. Turn under ¼" at the leg edge, fold up the hem allowance, and finish it by hand or machine, as you prefer.

Time to Retire

dults spend roughly a third of their lives asleep; children almost a half! Considering the amount of time children spend in their nightclothes, much less counting days spent home from school (sometimes with illnesses not quite as desperate as the description of the symptoms might indicate), sleepwear is an important part of their wardrobe.

Although children are rarely photographed in pajamas, how vivid can be our memories of them in pajamas . . . of shadows lengthening around sun-healthy bodies running across the lawn on mid-summer evenings; sweet, deep breathing as we check them before going to bed ourselves; bathrobes on Christmas morning and, when company comes, their coming downstairs all scrubbed and shiny, ready for bed, ready for a good-night kiss, a last look under the bed, a trip to the bathroom, a kiss for the teddy bear. . . .

Children's nightclothes rarely reflect cosmic vibrations of high fashion. Just as it was with the original drop-seat Dr. Denton's, the aim is still comfort, warmth, and washability. Styles are loose, fabrics stick to basics. Major concessions to fashion usually confine themselves to images of TV favorites and stylistic sports uniforms to fuel dreams of glory for the boys. Variety is achieved mostly with trims and color accents. For example, even though the boy's and girl's robes in this chapter are cut from the same basic pattern, the choice of fabric and the detailing of piping, lace, and pockets change the look completely. *Vive la différence!*

The traditional method of counting sheep to induce slumber seems to have worked for this young shepherd, caught just before the moment of awakening by an unknown eighteenth-century French artist painting in the style of François Boucher.

TECHNIQUES

Decorative Seams

These three decorative seams are design tools that can subtly emphasize the classic elegance of simple tailoring (piping outlines the traditional lines of the boy's robe), unify contrasting elements of design with repetition of color and trim (piping and lace unite the girl's robe with the nightie), or, as in the fagoted panel of the nightie, create a focal point for the eye and enhance the underlying beauty of a fabric or print with a delicate web of color.

1. The Piped Seam.

PREPARATION. Tear the piping fabric horizontally to establish a true grain. Fold the torn edge diagonally to meet one selvage and draw a pencil line parallel to the diagonal fold.

Unfold the fabric and, using the pencil marking as the diagonal grain line, measure and mark cutting lines spaced 1½″ apart, marking a line for each strip you wish to cut.

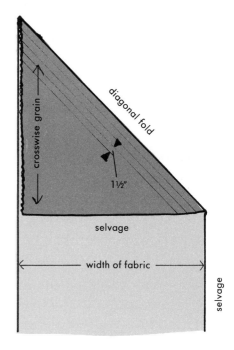

PIECING THE BIAS. Bias strips can be cut approximately one third longer than the width of the fabric. Thus the longest strip that can be cut from 45″-wide fabric is 60″. If the seam you want to trim is longer, you will have to piece together one or two shorter strips to achieve the desired length.

With right sides together, match and stitch the straight grain at the short ends, as shown.

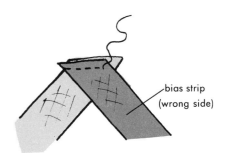

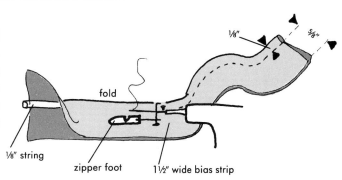

SEWING THE PIPING. With wrong sides together and raw edges aligned, fold the bias strip in half lengthwise. Put the zipper foot on the machine and stitch a length of ⅛″ wide preshrunk cording or postal string into the fold, maintaining a ⅝″ seam allowance on the right. Do not succumb to temptation and stretch the bias strip as you stitch, or the piping will curl.

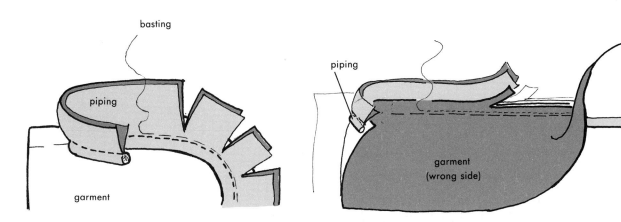

ATTACHING THE PIPING. The seam allowances of the garment and the piping strips may be unequal, particularly at collars and necklines. Match the stitching on the piping to the seam line of the garment. The raw edges should be aligned, but not necessarily flush.

Baste the piping to the right side of the piece to be trimmed, clipping the seam allowance of the piping and easing the fabric onto it, as necessary, to prevent stretching when rounding curves.

When stitching a piped seam, sandwich the piping between garment layers, keep the zipper foot on the machine, and stitch just inside the basting stitches which serve as a handy seam guide.

Trim all layers of the seam allowances separately to prevent them from making an ugly ridge when the seam is turned and pressed.

2. Garnishing the Piping with Lace. It is easier to see what you're doing if you baste the strips of lace over the piping, so plan ahead and choose to baste the trim to the garment or to the facing side of the seam so the lace won't hide the piping when the seam is turned.

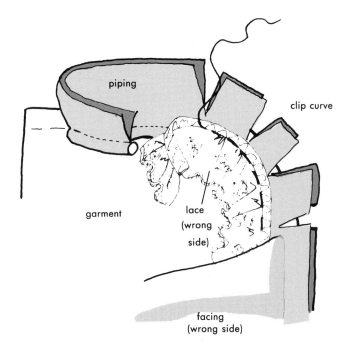

Once again, match seam lines (but not necessarily raw edges) as the seam allowance on the lace will most likely not match either the garment or the piping. Stitch the seam as before.

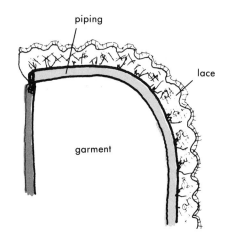

3. The Fagoted Seam.

DRAWING A STITCH DIAGRAM. Hem or face the raw edges that abut the seam.

Pencil the outline of the seam on a large piece of sturdy paper such as shelf paper or brown wrapping paper or non-woven interfacing, and then draw a second line parallel to the first, ⅛″ away. Connect the two lines with small cross bars, also spaced ⅛″ apart. When complete, the diagram should resemble a tiny set of railroad tracks.

Baste the abutting sides of the seam to the outlines of the diagram so that the cross bars are visible in between.

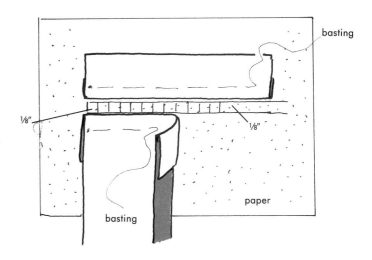

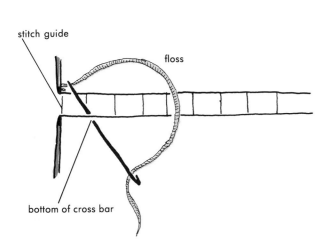

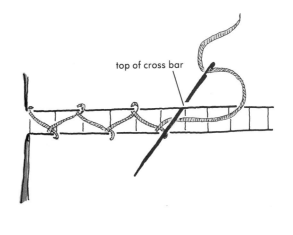

WORKING THE FAGOTING. Thread an embroidery needle with three strands of embroidery floss. Conceal your knot in the hem (or facing seam) at the *top* of the first cross bar on the left and take a small backstitch. Loop the thread to your right and, entering from the outside and emerging in the "ditch" with the needle pointing diagonally back toward the previous stitch, pick up the fabric at the *bottom* of the next cross bar to the right. Move one more cross bar to the right. Once again, entering from the outside and emerging in the ditch, take the next stitch at the *top* of the bar. This time the needle points diagonally down toward the previous stitch.

Complete the seam, moving one bar to the right with each stitch, alternating stitches at the tops and bottoms of the bars, always entering from the outside and emerging in the ditch with the needle pointing diagonally back toward the last stitch.

Fasten off with a back stitch or two, remove the basting, and lift the work from the diagram. "Set" the stitching with a little spray starch and a steam iron.

Boy's Plaid Bathrobe

Girl's Lace-Trimmed Bathrobe

Boy's Plaid or Girl's Lace-Trimmed Bathrobe

It's hard to believe that these two robes, which look so different, are made in the same way from the same pattern. In fact, the differences are so minimal that you can make the girl's robe simply by following the sewing instructions for the boy's robe and observing the specialized instructions given when differences occur.

Materials

2½ times the front pattern length of 60″-wide plaid or fleece fabric

½ yard 44–45″ contrast fabric for piping or twice the X–M length of purchased piping

Twice the X–M measurement ¾″-wide pre-gathered lace trim

The Grids

(If unfamiliar with the grid technique see page 180, or substitute any commercial pattern with a shawl collar and straight sleeves.)

Fold a grid and trace the pattern point-for-point and square-for-square, remembering to transfer any changes in the A–H line of the back pattern to the A–H line of the collar section of the front and front facing, as well.

Notice the dotted outline of the original sloper, the dropped armhole, and the flattened sleeve cap for ease of movement.

The shaded areas indicate extra width for ease of movement and extra length for an optional hemline.

If making the plaid robe, be sure to draw the horizontal plaid matching guidelines on the front, back, and facing patterns.

If making the girl's robe, use the full length allowance and the rounded pocket.

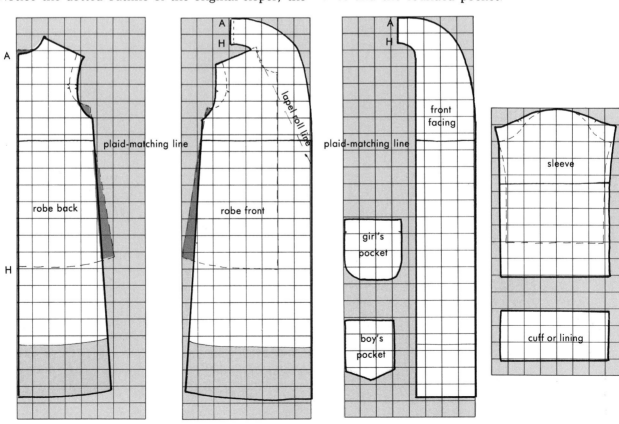

Layout and Cutting

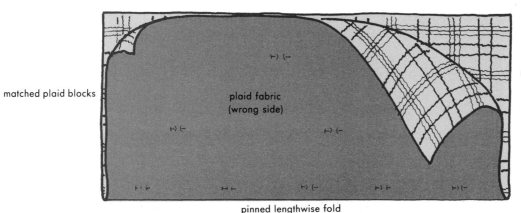

matched plaid blocks

matched plaid blocks

plaid fabric
(wrong side)

pinned lengthwise fold

1. *Matching Plaids.* It is important to analyze your plaid before matching it. Note how the wide and narrow vertical stripes, repeated thread-for-thread in the horizontal weave, intersect to form the characteristic squares of the plaid.

The Ogilvie plaid in the illustration has background squares of navy and green. The navy is accented with two, narrow, gold stripes; two navy pinstripes flank a single red stripe to punctuate the green. The plaid is balanced because it looks the same from right to left and from left to right.

Occasionally you will see a plaid that is not balanced (for instance, the small accent stripes might be navy, yellow, red, which would appear as red, navy, yellow,

when looked at from right to left). A really super matching job leaves the plaid block intact, giving an almost seamless appearance over straight seams and forming a perfectly matched chevron pattern at flared seams.

FOLDING THE FABRIC. Choose the center of one large block as a folding line, and fold the fabric in half vertically, right sides together. The selvages may or may not be flush, but they should be parallel.

Pin the fabric along the fold line to prevent shifting. Working from the center toward the selvages, pin the top layer to the bottom layer, periodically folding the top layer back to check the alignment of the plaid.

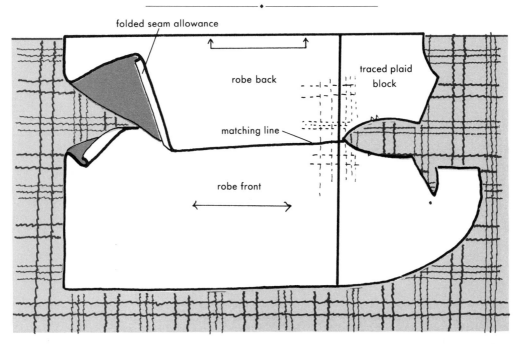

folded seam allowance

robe back

traced plaid block

matching line

robe front

CENTERING THE PLAID VERTICALLY. Place the center of the robe back pattern on the fold line so that the *hemline* falls at an attractive point in the plaid.

HORIZONTAL BALANCING. Seam lines rather than cutting lines are matched to prevent the seam allowances from swallowing up any part of the plaid block

161

that might be needed for horizontal symmetry. Fold under the side seam allowance and trace a square or two of the plaid onto the back pattern where the horizontal guideline intersects the side seam.

Similarly fold under the front side seam allowance and temporarily pin the front pattern next to the back pattern, seam lines touching at underarms and horizontal guidelines, and overlapping at the hem. Trace a few blocks of the plaid onto the front pattern, as you did the back, so you can check the continuity of the plaid across the seam line.

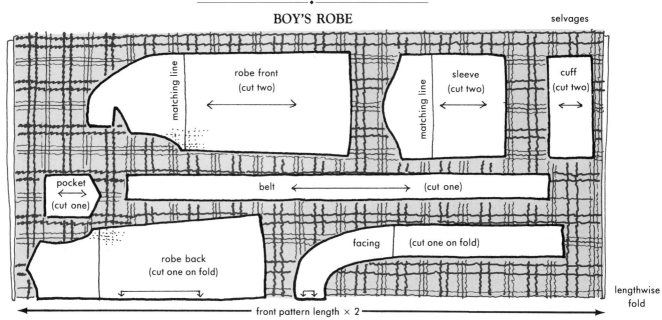

2. Laying Out the Pattern.

THE FRONT AND BACK. Leave the back pinned to the fabric. Unpin the front and relocate it, matching the traced plaid stripe-for-stripe and square-for-square at the new location. Return the side seam allowances to normal position before cutting.

THE SLEEVE. Lay the vertical grain line in the center of a block of plaid and match the horizontal grain line to the front and back.

THE FACING, CUFFS, POCKET, AND BELT. Match the front facing to the front lapel, and the cuff facing to the sleeve stripe-for-stripe and square-for-square. Match the pocket to the front, and cut the belt to show one full square when sewn.

GIRL'S ROBE. Follow the general layout of the illustration as your fabric width and pattern size permit.

GIRL'S ROBE

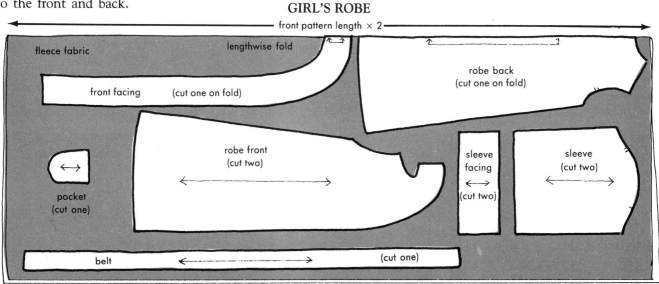

Sewing the Robe

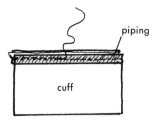

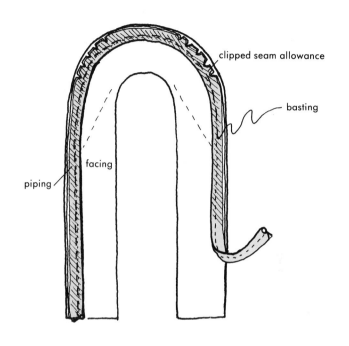

1. Preparing the Trim.

THE PIPING. Cut a length of piped trim (which you can buy, or sew according to the technique given in this chapter) to fit the outer curved edge of the lapel facing.

With right sides together and seam lines matching, baste and stitch the piping to the facing, starting at bottom right and ending at bottom left.

Ease the facing onto the piping around the neck curve, clipping the piping seam allowance as necessary. The raw edges of the piping and the facing should be parallel but not necessarily flush, as the seam allowances may differ.

Similarly prepare the cuffs.

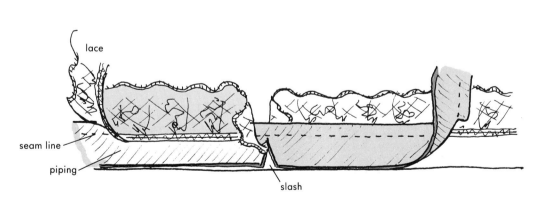

ADDING THE LACE. If you plan to use lace, baste it to the facings before adding the piping, matching seam lines rather than raw edges.

When trimming the lapel, the positions of the piping and the lace are reversed around the neck section so the lace won't hide the piping after the facing rolls to the outside and becomes the shawl collar.

Start at bottom left and baste the lace on top of the piping only to the level of the notch at the beginning of the roll line. At this point, slash the seam allowance of the piping right up to the stitching that holds the cord, pull the lace through the slash so the piping is on the top, and continue around the neck section, with piping on top and lace underneath, until you reach the next notch.

Slash the seam allowance of the piping, pull the lace through to its original position, and finish trimming the lapel.

163

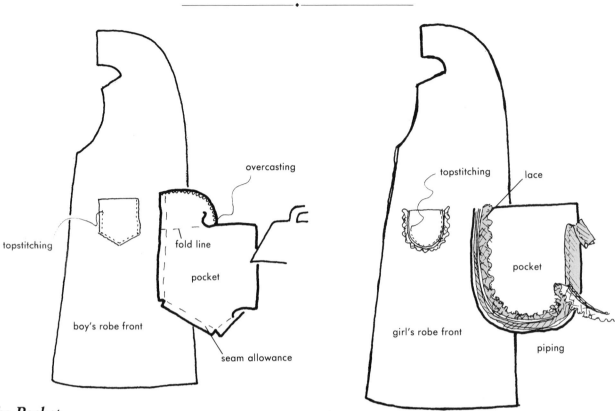

2. The Pocket.

BOY'S ROBE. The plaid pocket is not trimmed. Machine hem or overcast the top edge of the pocket. Press the seam allowances under at sides and bottom, and baste the pocket to the robe front (matching the plaid!) before topstitching.

GIRL'S ROBE. Similarly finish the top edge, and baste the lace and piping to the rounded edge before turning the seam allowances under and topstitching the pocket to the robe.

3. The Collar.

SHOULDER SEAMS. With right sides together, match the raw edges of the front and back shoulder seams. Ease the back onto the front and stitch the seam, starting at the armhole and stopping ¼″ from the neck edge.

Join the collar sections at center back and press the seam open.

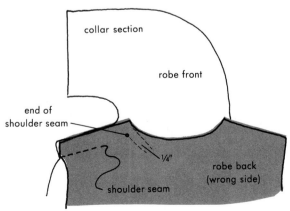

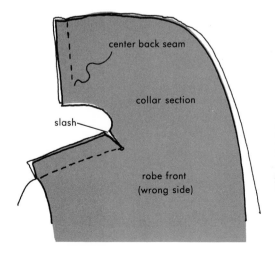

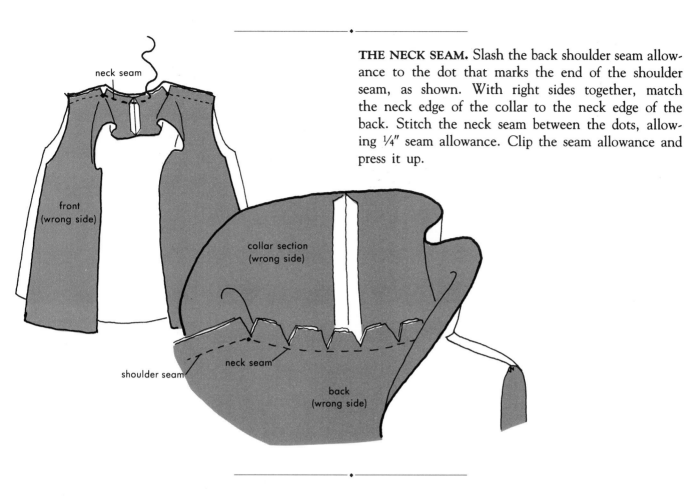

THE NECK SEAM. Slash the back shoulder seam allowance to the dot that marks the end of the shoulder seam, as shown. With right sides together, match the neck edge of the collar to the neck edge of the back. Stitch the neck seam between the dots, allowing ¼" seam allowance. Clip the seam allowance and press it up.

JOINING THE FACING. Finish the inner edge of the lapel facing as you did the pocket top.

Pin the lapel to the robe, with right sides together and raw edges aligned, sandwiching the piping (and lace) in the middle. Stitch the seam using the basting stitches that hold the piping as a seam guide. Trim the layers of the seam allowance singly, turn and press.

Clip the facing to the shoulder seam line, hem the neck to the neck seam, and tack the inner edge of the facing to the shoulder seams before turning the collar to the outside along the roll line.

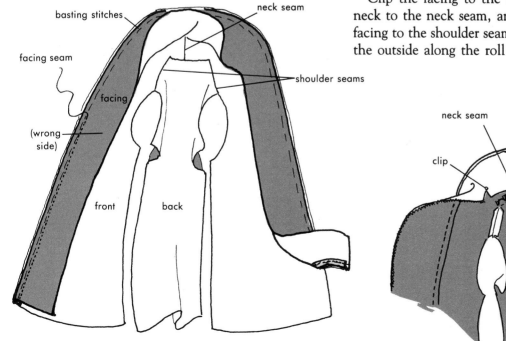

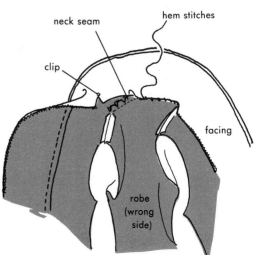

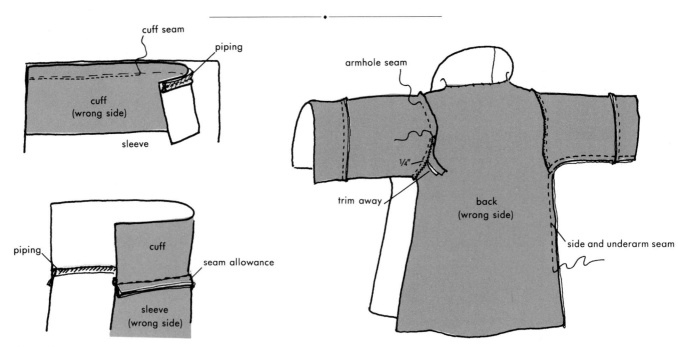

4. The Sleeves.

BOY'S ROBE.

THE CUFF. Stitch the trimmed cuff facing to the bottom of the sleeve and press the seam allowance up toward the sleeve.

THE ARMHOLE, SIDE, UNDERARM, AND CUFF SEAMS. Set the sleeve into the armhole. Overcast and trim the seam allowance to ¼". Close the side, underarm, and cuff facing in one continuous seam. Turn the cuff facing to the inside and hand or machine hem it to the sleeve.

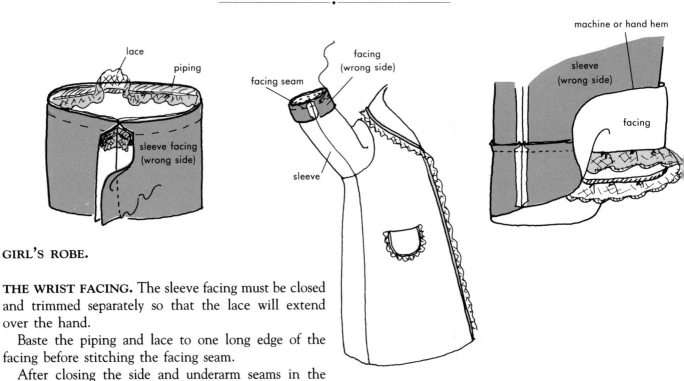

GIRL'S ROBE.

THE WRIST FACING. The sleeve facing must be closed and trimmed separately so that the lace will extend over the hand.

Baste the piping and lace to one long edge of the facing before stitching the facing seam.

After closing the side and underarm seams in the long, continuous seam, slip the facing over the sleeve, right sides together, and stitch them.

Finish the remaining long edge of the facing and hem it to the inside of the sleeve, as before.

5. Finishing the Robe.

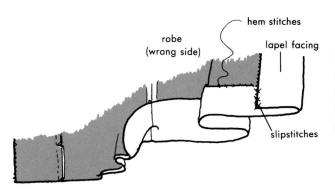

THE HEM. Open out the lapel facings and clip a wedge from the seam allowances at the hemline. Turn up the hem and finish it by hand or machine. Turn the lapel facings to the inside and secure them with a few slip-stitches.

THE BELT. Fold the belt in half lengthwise, right sides together, and seam the edges, leaving an opening in the middle of one long edge for turning the belt.

Clip the corners, turn the belt, and close the opening with slipstitches.

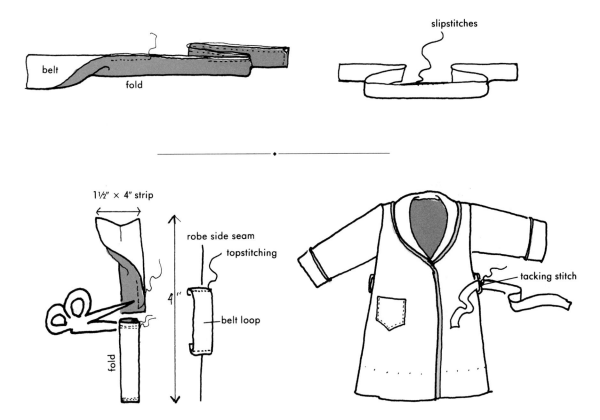

THE BELT LOOPS. Cut a 1½″ × 4″ strip of fabric. Fold it in half lengthwise, right sides together, and seam it ¼″ from the cut edges. Turn and press.

Cut the strip in half. Finish the raw ends with two closely spaced rows of topstitching.

Turn the finished ends under and topstitch the loops over the side seams at waist level.

A handy trick to keep track of the belt: Try on the robe, tie the belt, pin it, and later tack it to one of the loops at the side seam.

Girl's Nightie

This little nightie can be made with short sleeves for summer or long sleeves for winter. The fit is loose and the look is angelic; possibly misleadingly so, in some cases.

Materials

46″-wide printed cotton or flannel: Long sleeve: 2½ times shoulder-to-hem measurement of front nightie pattern (three lengths, if back nightie is cut on center fold of fabric)
Short sleeve: double the front measurement

1 yard of ¾″-wide lace edging

½ yard of ¼″-wide elastic

One skein of six-strand embroidery floss in accent color

The Grids

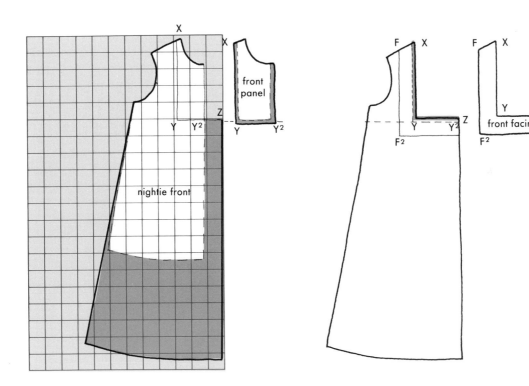

(If unfamiliar with the grid technique see page 180, or substitute any commercial pattern with simple A-line styling and long sleeves.)

THE FRONT GRID. Fold the appropriate grid. Trace the diagram point-for-point and square-for-square, noticing the outline of the original shift sloper and the shaded areas that include a six-square hem extension, a one square extra ease allowance at the side seam, and a one-square gathering extension at center front below the styleline.

STYLING THE PANEL. Line X–Y–Y²–Z is the style-line that separates the front panel pattern from the nightie pattern. Draw the line and cut the pattern apart. Tape paper under the cut edges so that you can add a ¼″ seam allowance outside points X–Y–Y² on the panel and inside points X–Y–Y²–Z on the nightie, as indicated by the dotted lines.

THE FACING. Notice the facing outline F–F²–F³–Y²–Y–X, and trace that also, similarly adding seam allowances, as shown.

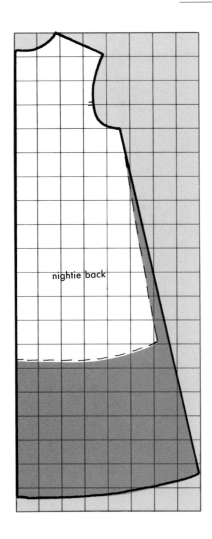

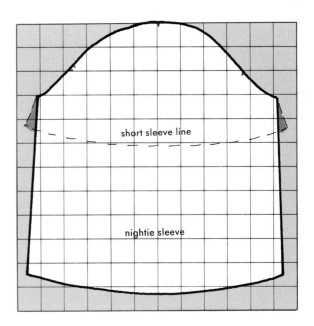

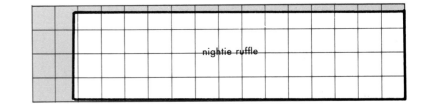

THE BACK. Fold another grid and trace the back pattern point-for-point and square-for-square, also including the shaded areas where the basic shift sloper has been modified for the design.

THE SLEEVE. Fold the appropriate grid and similarly trace your choice of the long- or short-sleeve pattern.

THE RUFFLE. Trace one 11 × 3½ square ruffle rectangle.

Layout and Cutting

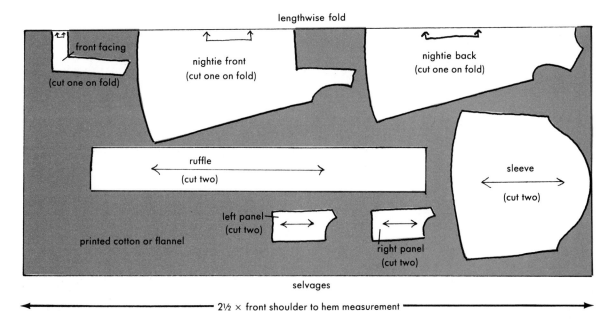

lengthwise fold

front facing

(cut one on fold)

nightie front
(cut one on fold)

nightie back
(cut one on fold)

ruffle
(cut two)

sleeve

(cut two)

left panel
(cut two)

right panel
(cut two)

printed cotton or flannel

selvages

2½ × front shoulder to hem measurement

Fold the fabric in half lengthwise, wrong sides together, and lay out the pattern pieces according to the general principles of the sample layout, being sure to align the arrows with the lengthwise grain and placing all fold symbols against the lengthwise fold.

Sewing the Nightie

1. Assembling the Front.

THE NIGHTIE CUTOUT. The center of the cutout needs three rows of gathering stitches: the first on the seam line, the second ⅛″ within it, and the third ⅛″ outside it on the nightie itself. (Don't worry that the third row will show; it will be hidden by the lace trim. But it does help hold the gathers attractively in place after turning the facing to the inside.)

Imitate the look of hand sewing with very light upper-thread tension and approximately 14 stitches to the inch.

THE FACING. Zig zag an overcasting ¼″ away from the outer edges of the facing. Use the widest stitch setting, 14 stitches per inch, and very light upper-thread tension to best approximate the look of commercial overcasting. After sewing, trim the excess seam allowance to the edge of the overcasting.

THE FACING SEAM. Pull up all three gathering rows until the nightie fits the facing. Sew all three sides of

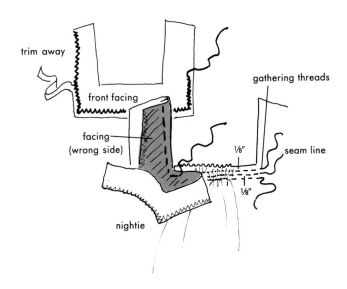

trim away

front facing

gathering threads

facing
(wrong side)

⅛″

seam line

⅛″

nightie

the cutout to the facing, with right sides together and raw edges aligned, using the center gathering row as a stitching guide across the bottom of the square. Clip the corners, turn the facing to the inside, and press.

171

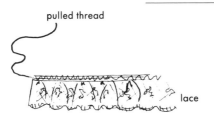

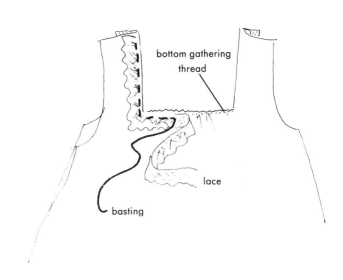

THE LACE. Cut a length of lace approximately one third longer than the perimeter of the cutout. Pull one of the straight woven threads in the long top edge, gathering the lace slightly until it fits exactly. Baste the gathered lace, right side up, to the right side of the cutout, allowing a slight extra fullness at the corners to prevent the lace from curling upward over the panel later.

2. The Fagoting.

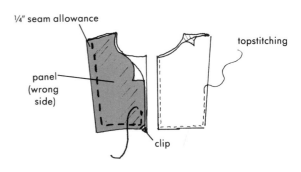

PREPARING THE PANELS. Match the right and left front panels to the facings, with right sides together and raw edges aligned. Leaving the neck and shoulder edges open, seam the three outer edges observing the ¼″ seam allowance.

Clip the corners diagonally, turn the panels right side out, and press. Stabilize the shape of the completed panels with topstitching, as shown.

DRAWING THE STITCH GUIDE. Pin the prepared nightie to a piece of paper or non-woven interfacing that completely fills in the cut-out opening with at least 2″ to spare on all sides. Draw the outline of the cutout onto it with a water-soluble embroidery transfer pen or light pencil that won't smudge. Remove the nightie and draw a second outline, ⅛″ away from and parallel to the first, inside it.

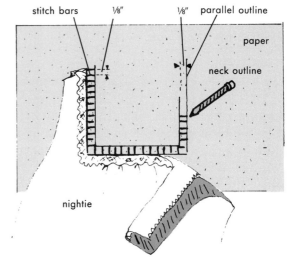

Connect the two outlines with cross bars spaced ⅛″ apart, just as if you were drawing a tiny railroad track, as described in "Techniques" at the beginning of this chapter. As you approach the corners, use your judgement to place the stitches evenly on both sides, deviating slightly from the ⅛″ spacing, as necessary.

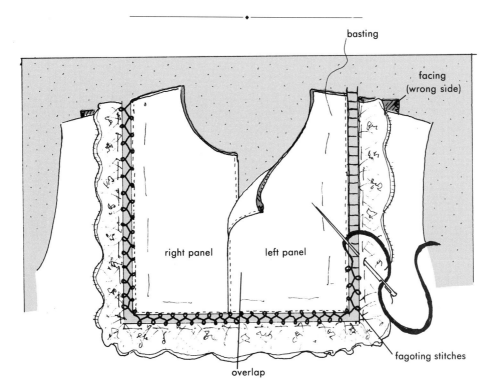

WORKING THE STITCH. Pin the nightie to the guide, aligning the edge of the cutout to the outer line. Pin the right and left panels inside the cutout following the inner line, permitting them to overlap at the center front. Secure all the pieces with large basting stitches and remove the pins which will infuriatingly snag the floss while you work the fagoting stitches.

Join the panels to the nightie with fagoting (following the instructions at the beginning of the chapter), completely piercing all thicknesses of the panels and catching the edge of the lace in every stitch on the nightie side.

3. The Neck.

THE SHOULDERS. Join the nightie back to the assembled front at the shoulders, finishing the seams in any way you prefer.

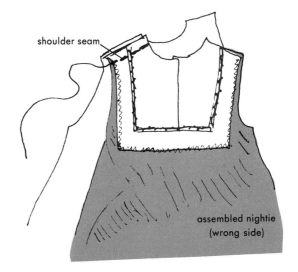

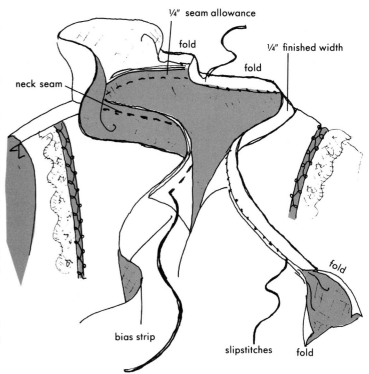

THE BINDING. Trim the neck edge of the nightie to the seam line so that the top fold of the binding will be positioned at the actual neckline rather than at the inner edge of the seam allowance, which would make the neck too small. Two neck strips were cut in the layout. Trim one to a width of 1″ and a length equal to one long edge of the ruffle. Discard the other or save it for trimming the robe.

Starting at the center back and working out toward the front, with right sides together and raw edges aligned, pin and seam the strip to the neckline. Maintain a ¼″ seam allowance, stretching the binding very slightly as you sew.

Fold the bias to the inside, turn in the remaining long edge, and hem it to the stitches of the neckline seam.

THE TIE EXTENSIONS. Fold in ¼″ seam allowances on all remaining raw edges of the tie extensions and secure them with topstitching or hand slipstitches.

4. The Sleeves.

THE HEM. Topstitch a narrow hem at the bottom of either the short or the long sleeve.

THE ELASTIC. Depending on the length of the sleeve you have chosen, cut a length of ¼″-wide elastic to comfortably fit the child's biceps or wrist. Sew two gathering rows spaced one square above the finished hem, and pull up the threads so that the gathered area is 2″ longer than the elastic. Zigzag the elastic to the wrong side of the sleeve on top of the gathering threads, stretching it uniformly as you sew.

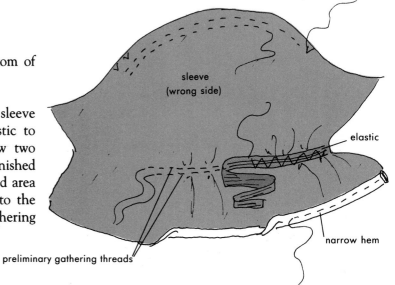

THE CAP. Similarly prepare the cap with two rows of gathering stitches between the notches. Pull up the gathers and pin the sleeve into the armhole, matching single notches in the front and double notches in the back. Stitch the armhole seam, finishing it as you did the shoulder seam.

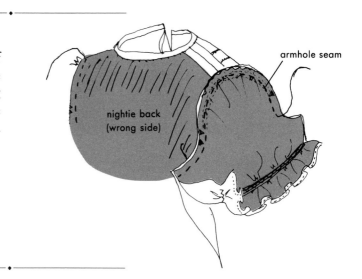

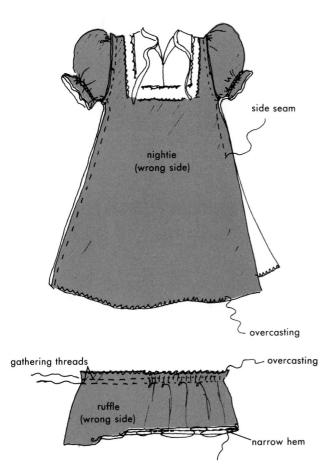

5. The Ruffle.

PREPARATION. Prepare the ruffle with a narrow top-stitched hem at the bottom and two rows of gathering stitches along the entire top edge.

JOINING THE RUFFLE TO THE NIGHTIE. Close the side and underarm seams of the nightie and overcast the raw edge at the hem. Overcast the top edge of the ruffle after pulling up the gathers to fit the bottom of the nightie, and seam the short ends together.

Pin the assembled ruffle to the bottom of the nightie, with right sides together and raw edges aligned, allowing the customary ⅝″ seam allowance.

Try it on. If you are satisfied with the length, stitch the ruffle as is. If there is room for a growth allowance, move the ruffle upward until it reaches the desired level. (The seam allowance of the nightie will now be deeper than the seam allowance of the ruffle.) Stitch the seam with long machine stitches that will be easy to remove when you are ready to lower the ruffle next year.

A Library of
Pattern Shapes

hildren, and for that matter adults, vary tremendously in body size and shape. Picture for a moment, a class of school children, some as tall as string beans, towering over their medium-sized classmates, with a liberal sprinkling of roly-poly elves to complete the scene. But even as children differ individually, they also differ from themselves in that most of them experience several different body sizes and shapes in the course of growing up. Picture now the child you knew as a chubby three-year-old, hardly bigger than that chocolate ice-cream cone (traces of which can be found on the cheeks and the clothing outside the tummy), transformed six years later into a spindly, freckle-faced rascal with Band-Aids on both knees, grinning in the sun at summer camp.

Amazingly, no matter how the proportions of children of disparate ages and sizes may vary certain body ratios remain constant to us all, particularly those ratios involving the spine. You may remember from high-school biology that the spinal column is composed of three continuous groups of vertebrae. Five, closely-packed cervical vertebrae form the neck and support the head; seven thoracic vertebrae form the backbone and support the rib cage; five lumbar vertebrae lie below the waist at the base of the spine. The collarbone extends from the top of the rib cage at shoulder level, and the shoulder blade, hanging from the back of the collarbone, supports the muscle groups that move the arm. In most people, the bottom of the shoulder blade is level with the seventh thoracic vertebra. Therefore, clothing must be planned so that the armhole is at

This crowd, enjoying a day at the beach at the turn of the century, provides ample opportunity for comparing body proportions and relationships.

that approximate level, to allow free movement of the arm. The waist falls at the bottom of the rib cage, level with the last thoracic vertebra. The distance from waist to armhole is approximately three fifths of the overall waist-to-neck length at the center back.

Because the spine grows as a continuous unit, the relationship of the vertebrae to each other and to the shoulder blade remains the same, even though the relationship to the head, length of leg, and girth, may vary enormously. Toddlers, for instance, are round with short legs, bulky diapers, and a proportionately larger head than eight-year-olds who have begun to grow taller and have longer legs in comparison to head size and girth.

Some other proportions also remain constant. The tiniest newborn and the biggest weight lifter (assuming both have the normal number of vertebrae) will have elbows coinciding with waist level and wrists at hip level when the arm is at rest against the side.

The more nimble among you can try a simple experiment that illustrates a curious (and totally useless) example of body relationships. Sit down and remove your shoes. Flex your left elbow. Cross your legs, and, swinging the right leg over until the sole of your foot rests against the inside of your left forearm, tuck your heel into the crook of the bent elbow. Your toes most likely will extend far enough beyond your wrist to touch your curled fingers.

Drafting the Patterns

A few of the child's own measurements combined with the formulas of body relationships will enable you to develop a basic set of patterns (called *slopers* in the garment industry) to fit any child and adapt to all the projects in this book.

No set of generalities, of course, can fit every child, even considering the traditionally easy-going attitudes about the fit of children's clothes. You may have to go back to the drawing board several times before achiev-

ing a really good fit on the first pattern. But the effort will be worth the time. When the first sloper is perfected you will have created the basis for everything else you want to try—including subsequent slopers or experimenting with your own designs—with no need for deciphering complicated measurement tables, expertise in patternmaking, or specialized drafting equipment.

---

1. Tools.

Continuous roll of 20"-wide paper: shelf paper, brown wrapping paper, etc.

Transparent ruler, 2" × 18"

3H pencil

Artist's eraser

Paper scissors

Sheets of 18" × 24" poster board, bristol board, or oaktag

Dressmaker's tracing wheel

36"- or 42"-wide unbleached muslin, medium weight

Sewing pins

Soft pencil or washable fabric pen for marking fabric

---

2. Measuring the Bodice. Dress the child in a snug T-shirt or leotard. Hang a necklace around the neck and tie a string or length of yarn around the waist. Thick yarn, least likely to slip, is an advantage for younger children who generally have fat little tummies instead of waists! Record the following measurements on a piece of paper:

BACK SHOULDER TO WAIST. Going down over the shoulder blade, measure from the intersection of the shoulder seam and the necklace to the waist string.

CENTER BACK. Measure the length of the spine from the necklace to the string.

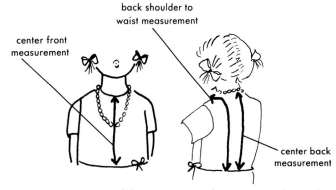

CENTER FRONT. Measure over the tummy from the hollow of the neck to the waist string.

WAIST. Snip the string without untying the bow and measure the string to determine the waist measurement.

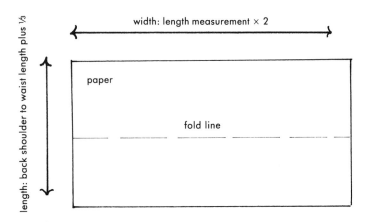

width: length measurement × 2

length: back shoulder to waist length plus ⅓

paper

fold line

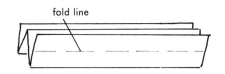

(size of square determined by your measurements or average measurements in Quick Grid Appendix p. 191)

fold line

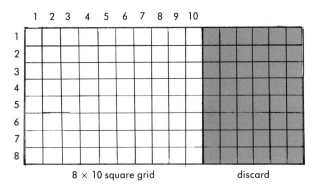

8 × 10 square grid   discard

3. Transferring Bodice Measurements to a Paper Grid.

THE BASIC SQUARE. Compute the *back shoulder to waist* measurement into thirds. (If you prefer the ease of working with multiples of ten, compute your measurements in centimeters which are also marked on modern tape measures.) Cut a large piece of your pattern paper into a rectangle using the *back shoulder to waist* measurement *plus one third* for the length. Double this measurement for the width.

FOLDING THE GRID. Fold the paper in half horizontally, then in quarters, then in eighths, making very sharp, straight creases. When unfolded, the paper will be divided into eight sections separated by seven creases. Similarly fold the paper in half vertically and

repeat the folding procedure: quarters, eighths, and finally sixteenths, until you have folded an 8 × 16 square grid. Trim away the shaded 6 × 8 square grid and save it for another time. Starting in the upper left hand corner, number the vertical and horizontal crease lines of the remaining 8 × 10 square grid, as shown. Record the size of the square for convenience in folding future grids.

4. Drawing the Bodice Pattern.

FEATURE POINTS. Locate the following points on your grid:
  A Intersection of neck and center back or front.
  B Intersection of neck and shoulder.
  C Intersection of shoulder and armhole.
  D Mid-armhole.
  E Intersection of armhole and side seam.
  F Intersection of side seam and waist.
  G Princess point.
  H Intersection of waist and center back or front.

CONNECTING THE POINTS. Using the 3H pencil, locate and dot the feature points on back and front grids, connecting them following the illustration point-for-point and square-for-square, making sure to have 90 degree angles at A, E, F, H.

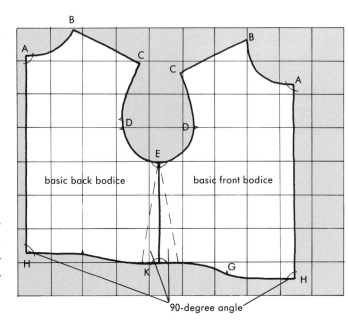

basic back bodice   basic front bodice

90-degree angle

SHAPING THE WAIST. Locate points K, spacing them ½" from point F.

SEAM ALLOWANCE. The varying seam allowances at neck and shoulder may seem unusual to you. However, because they absorb many of the minor differences in proportions that occur when enlarging patterns, they are actually the key to the grid system of grading. Mark the seam allowances within the front and back outlines as follows:

Neck: A–B = ¼"
Shoulder: B–C = ¾"
All others: ⅝"

SEPARATING THE PATTERNS. Cut out the paper patterns following points A–B–C–D–E–F–G–H. Do not cut the waist shaping at point K until you have fitted the bodice.

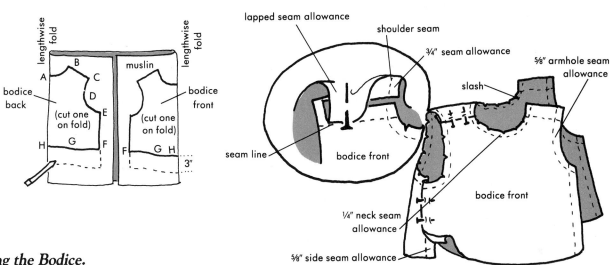

5. Fitting the Bodice.

CUTTING OUT. Cut a full width of muslin 4" longer than the B–G measurement. Gate fold the fabric lengthwise so the selvages meet in the center. Place the center front and center back of the patterns along the left and right folds, as shown. Draw a hemline directly onto the muslin 3" below and parallel to the H–G–F curve. Cut the front and back from the muslin including the extra hem allowance.

PINNING. Fold one of the back shoulder seam allowances to the inside and lap it over the front shoulder seam allowance, with seam lines flush. Pin designer-style, placing the pins about 1" apart at 90-degree angles to the seam line. Let the extra ¼" ease in the back shoulder ripple into the center.

Similarly pin the side seam from point K to the underarm.

Release the inner curve of the neck and armhole seam allowances with small slashes at 90 degrees to the seam line, spaced ½" apart.

Slip the bodice over the child's head and pin the remaining shoulder seam. Put the bodice on the child and tie another string around the waist. Mark the level of the waist on the muslin, ½" below the string.

6. *Judging the Bodice Fit.*

IF IT LOOKS RIGHT. If it looks right, it probably is right. The bodice should "sit" well on the shoulders, the waist gently gathered into the string.

Resist the temptation to overfit, particularly in the underarm and side seam areas. Active children need plenty of ease in their clothes, especially when sleeves are added. Darts can always be sewn in the front waist for fitted styles. Even then, the back waist usually hangs free or is gathered into a sash; and, anyway, children's clothing rarely depends on couturier fit for its charm!

IF IT LOOKS WRONG. If it looks wrong, unfortunately, it probably *is* wrong. The grids are based on industry measurements for size three, so that size probably will need the least fixing. The neck will tend to become proportionately larger in the bigger sizes, and the chest too small in the smaller sizes. Fortunately, corrections are easily made.

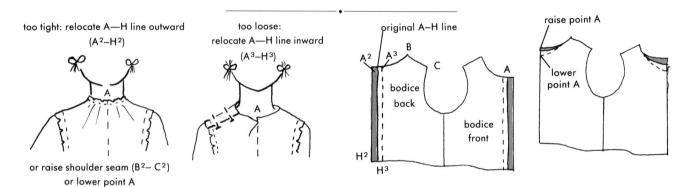

THE NECK. The neck should fit comfortably at the seam line without pulling, tugging, or gaping. Wrinkles radiating outward from the neck are a sure sign that it is too tight. Did you slash the seam allowance? You may further remedy neck fit problems by increasing or decreasing the seam allowances at the shoulder (point B) or relocating the center front and back (A–H) lines.

Changes should be cautiously approached. Even seemingly insignificant changes can have cumulative effects. For instance, moving the A–H lines in or out by as little as $\frac{1}{16}''$ can increase or decrease the total neck measurement by as much as $\frac{1}{4}''$. Sometimes you can successfully fit the neck simply by lowering point A and reshaping the curve.

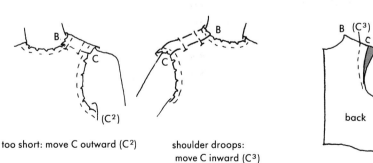

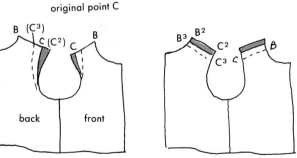

THE SHOULDER. Most commonly, the shoulder will be droopy. Check the neck fit first. If that is satisfactory but the end of the shoulder seam is clearly drooping over the arm, relocate point C so that the raw edge of the bodice is $\frac{1}{2}''$ inside the point where the arm begins to drop from the shoulder. Conversely, relocate point C outward if the shoulder seam is too short. Redraft the B–C line and the C–D–E armhole curve on bodice front and back.

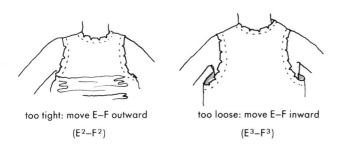

too tight: move E–F outward
$(E^2\text{–}F^2)$

too loose: move E–F inward
$(E^3\text{–}F^3)$

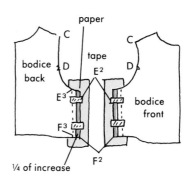

THE CHEST. Allow plenty of ease for movement, growth, and setting sleeves. If it's absolutely necessary to enlarge or diminish the chest circumference, relocate the E–F line. When moving the E–F line outward to enlarge the bodice, tape a paper extension to the sides of back and front bodices. Compute one fourth of the total desired increase and relocate points E and F on the paper. When decreasing the chest measurement, simply move points E and F inward. Redraft the C–D–E armhole curve, being sure not to change the vertical location of point E.

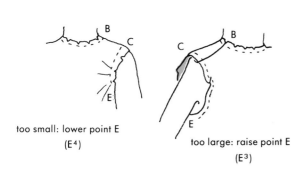

too small: lower point E
(E^4)

too large: raise point E
(E^3)

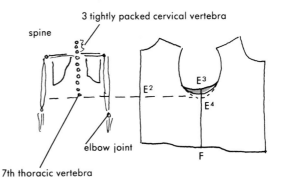

THE ARMHOLE. Rarely will the armhole depth give trouble. Again, wrinkles radiating from it are trouble signs. Did you slash the seam allowance? If so, minor adjustments can be made in the shoulder seam at point C. Increase the seam allowance to tighten the armhole; release it to gain more ease.

If all else fails, you must raise or lower point E so that it is roughly equal to the level of the seventh thoracic vertebra. Locate this by counting down from the neck-lace. There will be three cervical vertebrae bunched together at the top of the spine, above the thoracic vertebrae, which are more widely spaced. Count ten in all and mark the level directly on the muslin. Label it point E^2. Locate point E^2 on the pattern and draw a horizontal line across the bodice pattern at this level. Relocate point E at the intersection of the E^2 line and the side seam line E–F.

183

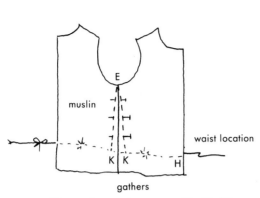

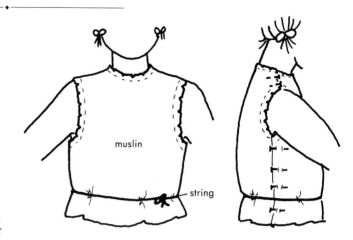

THE WAIST. Draw the waist curve K–G–H onto the grid so that it matches the pencil line on the muslin. If more than 3″ was gathered into the string across the front bodice, reshape the E–K line as necessary, remembering to divide the shaping equally between the front and the back.

Sometimes the whole thing is simply too big or too small. Check your measurements: you may need to enlarge or diminish the size of the grid itself.

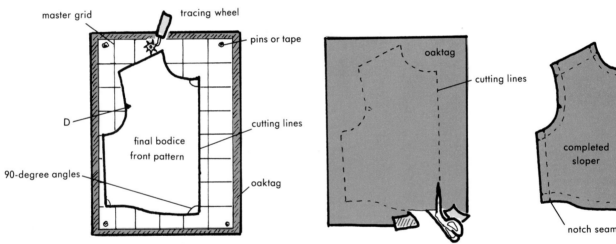

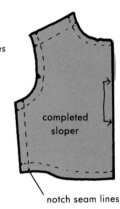

7. Finishing the Pattern.

THE FINAL DRAFT. Carefully translate all of the correct measurements from the muslin to the master grid, relocating any feature points that may have been changed. Indicate point D with a single notch in the front and a double notch in the back.

SEAM ALLOWANCES. Redraft seam allowances wherever feature points have been relocated.

TRUEING THE LINES. True all the lines in the final pattern by tracing over them with the ruler, extending them well beyond the feature points to insure accuracy and crisp angles at crossings. Label the pattern with the child's name and date and throw all the earlier versions away!

STABILIZING THE SLOPER. The paper draft needs to be transferred to sturdier stock in order to withstand frequent use. Tape or pin the sheet of oaktag to a flat work surface, then tape or pin the final pattern securely on top. Roll the tracing wheel over the **cutting** lines of the pattern using enough pressure to make perforated lines in the oaktag underneath. Remove the paper and cut the oaktag along the perforated outlines of the pattern to create a convenient set of stencils which will enable you to quickly trace innumerable copies of the original when developing the project patterns in the book or working out your own design ideas.

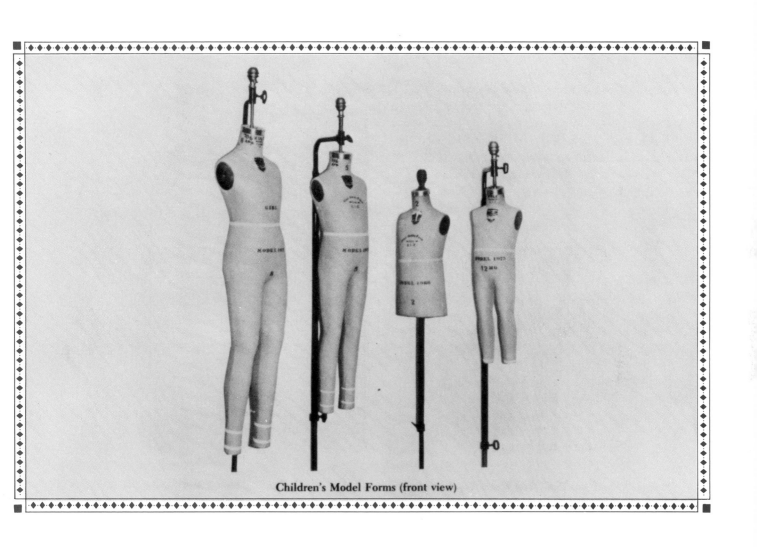

Children's Model Forms (front view)

A group of children's dress forms used to develop patterns in the industry.

Developing Additional Slopers

Once the basic bodice is fitted and the sloper stencil is made, the slopers for sleeve, shift, and pants follow naturally. All are based on grids folded from the same basic square as the bodice and are drafted and finalized in the same way.

1. The Master Pattern.
It will help you to have a permanent record of any changes made.

Fold a grid and trace the original bodice just as illustrated on pages 180–182.

Lay your finished sloper stencil over the original, matching all points that have not been changed.

Trace the outline of your finished sloper on top of the original, but in a different color pencil. You then have a permanent record of both for comparison and will be able to automatically transfer any alterations to the grids when developing additional slopers and making patterns for the projects.

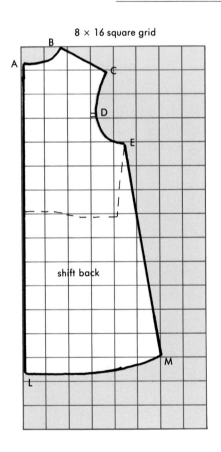

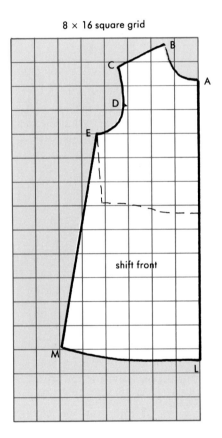

2. The Shift Sloper.

FOLDING THE GRID. For ease in folding, all grid sizes are based on a number of squares with a square root of four. Using the dimensions of the square you developed for the basic bodice, cut a piece of paper large enough to fold an 8 × 16 square grid. Fold the paper as necessary to complete the grid.

TRACING THE SLOPER. Place the back sloper stencil at the upper left side of the grid so that the feature points correspond to your master pattern. Trace the outline and identify points A, B, C, D, E, H; omit F, G. Locate points M and L six squares below the level of K and H, as shown.

Following the grid point-for-point and square-for-square, draw the A–H–M line, shape the hem curve M–L, and side seam E–L. If you have relocated points A–H or E, keep the A–M and E–L relationships the same as indicated on the grid.

THE FRONT SLOPER. Fold another 8 × 16 square grid and trace the outline of the front shoulder as you did the back. Similarly locate and connect points M and L.

SEAM ALLOWANCES. Extend the ⅝″ side seam allowance of the bodice to the hem and repeat all others exactly.

---

3. The Sleeve Sloper. The sleeve sloper is drafted without elbow ease. It will never be used as an actual sleeve but only as a guide for measurements such as cap height, overarm length, underarm length, elbow location, and circumference of biceps and wrist.

THE GRID. Fold an 8 × 8 square grid. Locate and connect points B–E^2–D^2–C–D–E–A. Mark ⅝″ seam allowances all around, except at the wrist. Draw double notches on the back sleeve at D^2 and a single notch to mark the front at point D.

GRAIN LINES. Vertical: Locate C^3 and connect points C–C^3. Horizontal: Connect E–E^2.

SHAPING THE CAP. Cut the sleeve pattern following B–C^3–A–E–D–C–D^2–E^2–B. Fold the sleeve in half

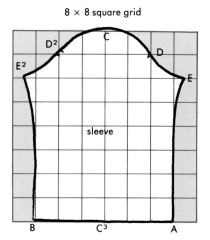

8 × 8 square grid

vertically along the C–C^3 line. Scoop out the E–D front armhole curve so that it is ¼″ deeper than the E^2–D^2 curve in the back. Mark ⅝″ seam allowances on all sleeve seams.

---

4. Fitting the Sleeve to the Armhole.

CUTTING THE MUSLIN. Cut a length of muslin 4″ longer than the back shift pattern. Fold it in half lengthwise, selvages matching. Place the back shift pattern 2″ away from the selvages. Extend the neck and hem curves to the selvage, as shown, to create a facing extension.

Place the front pattern on the muslin, aligning the center front flush with the fold. If your muslin is large enough and your pattern is small enough, place the sleeve pattern in between. If not, cut an additional length of muslin for the sleeve.

Draw 2″ hem extensions on the muslin at the bottom of the front and back shifts, as well as the sleeve, and cut out all the pieces.

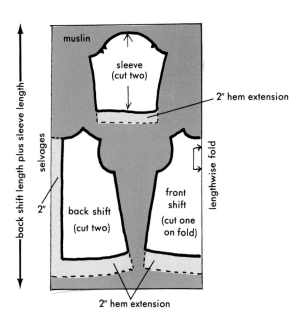

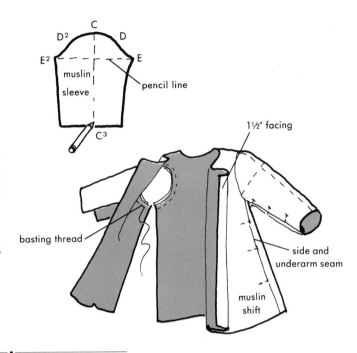

JOINING. Prepare the sleeve caps with two rows of gathering stitches between D and D^2. The first row should be on the seam line; the second, $\frac{1}{4}''$ away within the seam allowance. Draw the $C-C^3$ and $E-E^2$ lines on the muslin. Clip the neck and the armhole seam allowances and machine baste the shoulder seams together. Pull the gathers up over the cap and baste the sleeves into the armhole matching points $C-D-D^2$ and E. (The shift is fitted with both sleeves so that you can be sure it is properly balanced.) Pin the underarms and sides together in one continuous seam.

TRYING ON. Fold under and baste a $1\frac{1}{2}''$ facing at center back. Lap the right side over the left, allowing a $1''$ overlap. Pin closed from the outside.

5. Judging the Fit of the Shift.

THE SHIFT. Since the shift is drafted directly from the bodice it should fit without problems, especially if you have been careful to follow your final sloper exactly. Check that the A–H–M line hangs straight in the front, then mark and pin the hem at any desired level.

THE SLEEVE. The $C-C^3$ of the sleeve should flow evenly over the outside of the arm, and the horizontal lines at E should follow the body without serious distortion. Have the child bend her arm and mark the resulting crease in the muslin to establish the elbow height. With arm still bent, tie strings around the wrist and the upper arm at the desired short-sleeve level, as you did the waist. Mark the location onto the muslin with pencil, then cut the strings and measure them. Note the location and measurements of the strings on the paper pattern.

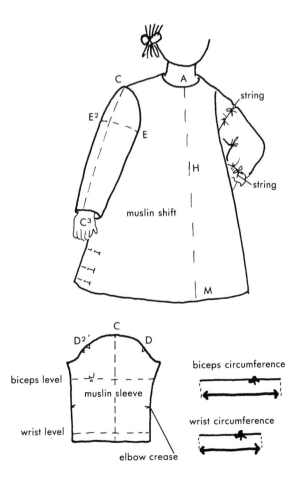

THE CAP. Ideally there should be $1''$ ease between D and D^2. However, since most children's sleeves are almost always cut with extra ease (puffed or gathered in some way but rarely fitted), this sloper will usually be satisfactory as is. If you still need to make corrections, increase or decrease the cap circumference as necessary by raising or lowering point C in $\frac{1}{4}''$ increments and reshaping the $D-C-D^2$ curve until the correct measurement is reached.

6. The Pants Sloper. A certain tolerance of fit always works to your advantage. Children's trousers are not usually expected to fit like designer ski pants but for comfort and hard wear. A fit that is anywhere near reasonable is considered adequate.

The pants sloper serves mainly to locate the level of the knee, ankle, and crotch. Notice that the crotch level on the grid is one third of the total length allowance. The variation to this rule is toddlers' bulky diapers. Add ⅛″ to the basic square measurement and include the shaded areas for extra fullness. This may not be completely accurate in every case, but chances are it will be close enough so that only minor adjustments need be made.

7. Drafting and Fitting the Pants Pattern.

THE GRID. Measure a piece of paper large enough to equal a 16 × 16 square grid, or two 8 × 16 square grids, depending on the size of your paper. Fold the paper in half, quarters, and eighths, until the grid is complete.

Trace the pants pattern onto the grid point-for-point and square-for-square, including the shaded squares for extra length allowance at the top, and including the shaded area at center back if your child still wears diapers.

Relocate the side seam (line C–D) and the center front or center back (line B–A) to correspond with any changes you have made in the bodice. Add ⅝″ seam allowance at the side seams if you have separated the pants front from the pants back along line C–D.

CUTTING OUT. Cut the pants from muslin, matching the arrows to the lengthwise grain, and adding an inch or two of hem allowance. Sew the inseams and the center front and center back seams, and pin the side seams if necessary.

Fit the pants as you did the sleeve, marking the knee and crotch creases that form when the child sits down, in order to establish the correct level of those points.

Use the string method to mark and measure the ankle and waist.

Correct the paper pattern as necessary.

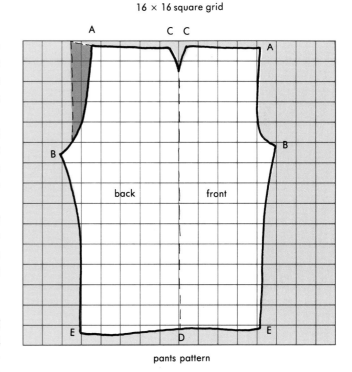

16 × 16 square grid

pants pattern

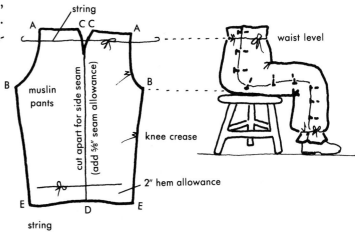

Appendix

Quick Grid Appendix

The size of the square is based on the average chest measurement in relation to average dress sizes. The pattern has added ease for movement and will be larger than the body measurement.

CHEST MEASUREMENT	DRESS SIZE	SIZE OF GRID SQUARE
21″	2	1½″ (3.8 cm)
22″	3	1⁹⁄₁₆″ (4 cm)
23″	4	1⅝″ (4.1 cm)
24″	5	1¹¹⁄₁₆″ (4.3 cm)
25″	6	1¾″ (4.5 cm)
26″	7	1¹³⁄₁₆″ (4.7 cm)
27″	8	1¹⁵⁄₁₆″ (4.9 cm)
28½″	10	2″ (5.1 cm)
30″	12	2⅛″ (5.4 cm)

Converting Inches to Centimeters

¼″ = .6 cm

⅜″ = 1 cm

½″ = 1.2 cm

¾″ = 1.8 cm

⅜″ = 1 cm

1″ = 2.5 cm

1½″ = 3.8 cm

2″ = 5.1 cm

3⅞″ = 10 cm

12″ = 30.5 cm

19¹¹⁄₁₆″ = 50 cm (½ meter)

36″ (1 yd.) = 91.4 cm

39″ = 100 cm (1 meter, or 1 M)

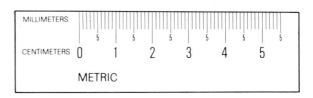

Mail Order Sources

If you have difficulty finding supplies in your locality the following mail-order sources carry many of the fabrics, patterns, notions, and trims mentioned in this book.

Smocking Information

SMOCKING ARTS GUILD OF AMERICA
BOX 75
KNOXVILLE, TN 37919
615 637-5456

Fine Fabrics and Laces;
Fine Sewing Information

MARGARET PIERCE INC.
1816 PEMBROKE ROAD
GREENSBORO, N.C. 27408
919 379-9542

Patterns and Smocking Supplies

LITTLE STITCHES
1115 BALMORAL ROAD
ATLANTA, GA 30319
404 255-5949

LITTLE MISS MUFFET
P.O. BOX 10912
KNOXVILLE, TN 37919

Stretch Fabrics and Notions

STRETCH AND SEW
7100 BROOKFIELD PLAZA
SPRINGFIELD, VA 22150
703 451-0155

Other Fabrics and Notions

G STREET FABRICS
11854 ROCKVILLE PIKE
ROCKVILLE, MD 20852
301 231-8998

Index

A

active play clothes, 90–125
  fabrics for, 91–93
  girl's bathing suit, 94–97
  girl's warm-up suit, 113–117
  hooded beach jacket, 98–102
  infant's "hippo bubble" romper, 118–125
  jogging suit, 103–108
  turtleneck jersey, 109–112
appliqué, 60, 77
armholes:
  fitting of, 183
  fitting of sleeve to, 187–188

B

bathing suits:
  boy's, 95
  girl's, 94–97
bathrobes, 158–167
batiste, 76
bloomers, 79–81
blouse, ruffle collar, 29–32
bodice:
  armhole fit of, 183
  chest fit of, 183
  fitting of, 181–184
  measurement of, 179–181
  neck fit of, 182
  shoulder fit of, 182
  waist fit of, 184
bonding, fusible, 93
bonnet, 132–136
boys' clothes:
  bathing suit, 95
  gingham shirt, 23–28
  jogging suit, 103–108
  plaid bathrobe, 158, 160–167
  smocked sunsuit, 143–151
  velvet jumpsuit, 57
  see also unisex clothes
bullion knot, 63
buttonholes, stretch, 93

C

cable stitch, 130
calico, 76
caps (of sleeves), 188
centimeters, inches converted to (table), 190
chain stitch, 62
chambray, 76
corduroy:
  how to sew, 20
  types of, 19
  velvet vs., 19
corduroy jumper, 38–43
corduroy overalls, 33–37
cotton, 75–76, 91
  types of, 76

D

dotted swiss, 76
double knit fabric, 92
dresses:
  girls', 46–53
  infants', 67–73

E

embroidery, 61, 69, 127
  stitches for, 62–63
  see also smocking
eyelet, 77

F

fabrics:
  knit (stretch), how to sew, 92–93
  mail order sources for, 191
  natural vs. synthetic, 91
  see also specific fabrics
facings, 93
fagoting, 157
French knot, 62

G

gingham, 19
  boy's shirt, 23–28
  how to sew, 21
  types of, 23
girls' clothes:
  bloomers, 79–81
  corduroy jumper, 38–43
  jogging suit, 103
  lace-trimmed bathrobe, 159–167
  nightie, 168–175
  princess slip, 86–89
  ruffle collar blouse, 29–32
  ruffled petticoat, 82–85
  smocked bonnet, 132–136
  smocked collar, 53–56
  smocked pinafore, 137–142
  stretch bathing suit, 94
  underwear, 74–89
  velvet party dress, 46–53
  warm-up suit, 113–117
  see also unisex clothes
grid system, 16–17, 190

H

half-step wave stitch, 131

hems, 21, 78
"hippo bubble" romper, 118–125
hooded beach jacket, 98–102

I

inches, centimeters converted to (table), 190
infant's dress, 67–73
infant's "hippo bubble" romper, 118–125
interfacing, 93

J

jackets:
  hooded, 98–102
  to jogging suit, 105, 107, 108
  to warm-up suit, 113–117
jersey, turtleneck, 109–112
jersey knit fabric, 92, 119
jogging suit, 103–108
jumper, 38–43
jumpsuit, 57–66

K

knit fabrics, how to sew, 92–93

L

lace, 77, 78, 163
lace-trimmed bathrobe, 159–167
lazy daisy, 62
linen, 91

M

mail order sources, 191

N

nightclothes, 153–175
  boy's bathrobe, 158, 160–167
  girl's bathrobe, 159–167
  girl's nightie, 168–175

O

open chain stitch, 62
organdy, 76
outline stitch, 130
overalls, 33–37

P

pants:
  bloomers, 79–81
  to jogging suit, 104, 106–107
  sloper for, 189

party clothes, 44–89
  bloomers, 79–81
  infant's dress, 67–73
  princess slip, 86–89
  ruffled petticoat, 82, 85
  underwear, 74–89
  velvet jumpsuit, 57–66
  velvet party dress, 46–53
patterns, 177–189
  for bodice, 179–184
  body ratios and, 177–179
  commercial, 16
  drafting of, 179–184
  grid system for, 16–17
  master, 186
  muslin, 16, 17
  for pants, 189
petticoat, 82–85
picture smocking, 131
pile fabrics, 19, 92
pinafore, 137–142
piping, 154–156
plaid bathrobe, 158, 160–161
plaids, matching of, 161–162
pleating machines, 129
princess slip, 86–89

Q

quadrille paper, 129

R

raglan sleeve shirt, 123, 124
ribbons, 93
rib knit fabric, 92
romper, 118–125
ruffled petticoat, 82–85

S

school clothes, 19–43
  corduroy jumper, 38–43
  corduroy overalls, 33–37
  gingham shirt, 23–28
  ruffle collar blouse, 29–32
seams, 20, 21, 77, 92, 124, 154–157
seed stitch, 63
shifts, 186–187, 188
shirts:

gingham, 23–28
  raglan sleeve, 123, 124
  turtleneck jersey, 109–112
silk, 91
sleeves:
  caps of, 188
  fit of, 188
  fitting of, to armholes, 187–188
  raglan, 123, 124
  sloper for, 187
slip, 86–87
slopers:
  for bodice, 179–184
  defined, 16, 179
  drafting of, 179–184
  pants, 189
  permanent, 17
  shift, 186–187
  sleeve, 187
  stabilizing of, 184
smocked bonnet, 132
smocked collar, 53–56
smocked pinafore, 137–142
smocked sunsuit, 143–151
smocking, 54–56, 119, 127–151
  basic, 128
  blocking of, 131
  function of, 127
  information and supplies, sources for, 191
  picture, 131
  pleating machines for, 129
  stitches for, 130–131
  techniques for, 129
  traditional, 131
  transfer dots for, 129
Smocking Arts Guild of America, 191
stem stitch, 130
stitches:
  embroidery, 62–63
  smocking, 130–131
stretch bathing suit, 94–97
stretch fabrics:
  how to sew, 92–93
  mail order sources for, 191

summer clothes with smocking, 127–151
    bonnet, 132–136
    pinafore, 137–142
    sunsuit, 143–151
sunsuit, 143–151

T
tape, buttonhole, 93
topstitching, 77–78
transfer dots, 129
turkey work, 63
turtleneck jersey, 109–112
two-step wave stitch, 131

U
underwear, 74–89

bloomers, 79–81
princess slip, 86–89
ruffled petticoat, 82–85
unisex clothes:
    corduroy overalls, 33–37
    hooded beach jacket, 98–102
    infant's dress, 67–73
    infant's "hippo bubble" romper, 118–125
    jogging suit, 103–108
    smocked bonnet, 132
    turtleneck jersey, 109

V
velour, 92
velvet:

corduroy vs., 19
matching nap of, 48
velour vs., 92
velvet party dress, 46–53
    smocked collar for, 53–56

W
wales in corduroy, 19
warm-up suit, 113–117
wave stitch, 131
wool, 91

Z
zig-zag sewing machine, 76, 92